Foundations of Modern Economics Series

Otto Eckstein, *Editor*

AMERICAN INDUSTRY:
STRUCTURE, CONDUCT, PERFORMANCE
Richard Caves

THE PRICE SYSTEM
Robert Dorfman

MONEY AND CREDIT: IMPACT AND CONTROL
James S. Duesenberry

LABOR ECONOMICS
John T. Dunlop

PUBLIC FINANCE
Otto Eckstein

ECONOMIC DEVELOPMENT: PAST AND PRESENT
Richard T. Gill

ECONOMIC SYSTEMS
Gregory Grossman

INTERNATIONAL ECONOMICS
Peter B. Kenen

NATIONAL INCOME ANALYSIS
Charles L. Schultze

PRENTICE-HALL, INC., ENGLEWOOD CLIFFS, NEW JERSEY

James S. Duesenberry

Harvard University

MONEY AND CREDIT: IMPACT AND CONTROL

PRENTICE-HALL
FOUNDATIONS OF MODERN ECONOMICS SERIES

Otto Eckstein, *Editor*

HG
181
.D76
(1)

PRENTICE-HALL INTERNATIONAL, INC., *London*
PRENTICE-HALL OF AUSTRALIA, PTY. LTD., *Sydney*
PRENTICE-HALL OF CANADA, LTD., *Toronto*
PRENTICE-HALL OF INDIA, PVT. LTD., *New Delhi*
PRENTICE-HALL OF JAPAN, INC., *Tokyo*
PRENTICE-HALL DE MEXICO, S. A., *Mexico City*

FOUNDATIONS
OF MODERN ECONOMICS SERIES

Economics has grown so rapidly in recent years that no one book can present it authoritatively today. *Foundations of Modern Economics* is a series of concise books surveying the major branches of the discipline, each written by a leading economist in the midst of the research and discussion of his specialty. Taken individually, each book reflects the structure, the content and the key scientific and policy issues of its field. The Series as a whole presents an account of Economics designed to be the material for the basic one-year college course.

Two of the nine books present the analytical core of Economics, *Price Theory* and *National Income Analysis.* Study of one or both of the core books is recommended before entering into the various fields of application. *Economic Development: Past and Present,* which uses a more historical approach, can be read without prerequisite and can serve as an introduction.

This new approach, as compared to the usual textbook, has several advantages. By mirroring the actual state of knowledge and discussion, the books gain in interest, depth, and relevance. They also communicate some of the excitement of the current research in a developing field.

The books free the teacher to devise his own course curriculum, rather than to follow the format of the textbook. Any selection or order of topics is possible once analytical principles have been mastered. Specific areas can be explored at greater length. The teacher not interested in a complete survey course can eliminate several of the books, spending more time on detailed study of a few fields. One-semester courses, emphasizing only micro-economics, or only macro-economics, can also be readily devised.

The books do not offer settled conclusions. They show the student the central problems of each field, and show how economic analysis permits more intelligent thinking about them. The Series is offered in the hope that this firsthand exposure will equip the student better as a citizen, and will attract him to the further pursuit of the subject.

Otto Eckstein, *Editor*

CONTENTS

MONEY AND CREDIT: IMPACT AND CONTROL

1

INTRODUCTION

Money is one of man's great inventions. Try to imagine the operation of a complex industrial society—especially a democratic one—without money. The fact that almost all but the simplest human societies have used money proves that it is an essential tool of civilization. But useful though it may be, money has always been a problem. Inflations and depressions have been the most serious problems of an industrial society—and defects in our monetary arrangements have played an important part in every major inflation and in every major recession we have suffered.

In their efforts to repair the apparent defects in their monetary arrangements, governments have erected elaborate systems of legislation to control the issue of currency and the operation of banks. Moreover, the victims of inflations, deflations, devaluations, and financial panics have understood that their troubles were in some way connected with the monetary system, but not exactly how. As a result, monetary disputes become disputes over articles of ideological faith. To most people "sound money" has the same standing as home and mother. But exactly which monetary policy is the "sound" one is not so well-agreed. And on the fringes of the debate there are always a few monetary cranks—the faith-healers of economics—who have found the one monetary system which will solve all the world's problems.

Why Money Is So Useful

Money is one of those things what we take for granted because it is difficult to imagine life without it. And it is so difficult for a complex society to exist without money that the breakdown of one monetary system is immediately followed by the development of a new one.

Money is essentially a device to permit people to exchange goods and services in a more convenient way than by direct barter. A moment's thought will convince you how difficult it would be to conduct an industrial economy by means of direct exchange of goods and services for goods and services. In a simple agricultural society each family may produce most of what it needs and little of what it does not need. A farmer can exchange small surpluses of food crops, or wood, or wool for the products of specialized artisans such as blacksmiths. The few specialists can re-exchange things they take in trade, if necessary. But that system works only when most families are almost self-sufficient. In a society where each person spends all his time producing one thing, or a part of one thing, almost everything produced must be sold; and many things are sold several times before they reach the final consumer. We manage to make all these trades because everyone is willing to accept money in exchange for any kind of good or service, in the confident expectation that he can use the money to buy any other kind of good or service. You can get an idea of the role money plays in our economy by noting how much it is used. The total volume of money transactions in 1960 was $4 *trillion*. About 60 per cent of the transactions were financial payments associated with trading in securities or other assets. The remaining 40 per cent—$1.5 *trillion* worth—were payments associated with the production, distribution, and consumption of goods and services.

Why Money Causes So Much Trouble

By using money we can divide the exchange process into two parts. It is a great deal easier to exchange goods and services for money, and then exchange the money for other goods and services, than to exchange one set of goods and services directly for another. But the fact that money enables us to break the exchange process into two parts is the source of a great deal of trouble. If goods can always be obtained for money, it always looks easy to get something for nothing—or for very little—by manufacturing money. For thousands of years monetary systems using metal coins were upset by counterfeiters, coin-clippers, or governments which tried to finance themselves by minting short-weight coins. With the development of paper money, the profitability of the private manufacture of bank notes and the efforts of governments to finance wars with paper money have produced numerous inflations, devaluations, and financial panics.

Breaking the exchange process into two parts causes another set of difficulties. In a barter world no one can sell goods or services without buying at the same time. When we use money it is possible to "sell now, buy later," meanwhile holding money. Ordinarily, anyone can do this without causing any harm. Usually, some people are increasing their holdings of money by selling more than they buy, while others are reducing previously acquired holdings. But when many people try to accumulate money at once, by selling without buying, there is trouble. Some other people find themselves unemployed or unable to sell what they have produced.

When people try to accumulate money by not spending what they receive, they do not add to the stock of money. But they do slow down the rate at which it moves. And when people try to reduce their holdings of money by spending more than they have received, the money doesn't disappear—it just moves faster. Unlike most things, money isn't used up when it's used.

When the amount of money in existence increases *or* when the rate at which money moves increases, there is more demand for goods and services. Within limits that's fine. Indeed, in an economy with a growing labor force and increasing productivity, we want the demand for goods and services to increase from one year to the next. But you can have too much of a good thing. If the flow of expenditures for goods and services increases very rapidly, the output of goods and services can't keep up and prices will have to rise.

On the other hand, if the amount of money decreases *or* if its rate of movement slows down, then prices, output, and employment will all decline.

Every major depression has been accompanied by a substantial decline in the money supply, and often by a complete collapse of the banking system. Among the many causes responsible for our major depressions, money and banking difficulties have always been prominent.

People have been using money for thousands of years and they've always had trouble with it. Sometimes people are complaining about inflation and blaming it on an excessive increase in the money supply. Sometimes the trouble is recession—unemployment, idle factories, and falling prices. Then they complain that the money supply is declining or not growing rapidly enough. There is seldom just the right amount of money circulating. A variety of devices for controlling the money supply have been tried in the last few hundred years. In the next two chapters we will trace the development of our changing monetary arrangements from the period of exclusive use of metal coin through the era of privately issued paper money down to the present system of control by the Federal Reserve System.

Control of Money As an Instrument of Economic Policy

It is easy enough to see that money is important to all of us and to see why, after centuries of experiments, we have made elaborate arrangements to control its supply in the public interest. But this only raises new questions about how that power is to be used.

The money supply influences expenditures for goods and services, and particularly investment expenditures. Through its impact on expenditures, the management of money affects four of the major objectives of economic policy: full employment, price stability, growth, and balance-of-payments equilibrium.

The Federal Reserve System influences expenditures for goods and services through its control over the money supply, although indirectly. Changes in money supply influence the behavior of banks and other lending agencies. The resulting changes in interest rates and the availability of credit then influence expenditures for business investment, construction of houses, and other types of spending.

In Chapters 3 and 4 we will study the impact of Federal Reserve policy on the behavior of banks. In Chapter 5 we will examine the behavior of other lenders and spenders who lend and borrow in the capital markets. In Chapter 6 we will see how interest rates are determined and how monetary policy can be used as a means of controlling expenditure and employment. In Chapter 7 we will review the practical effects of Federal Reserve policy. Finally, in Chapter 8, we can consider some of the problems and conflicts of objectives which make monetary policy a continuing subject of controversy.

2

THE NATURE AND EVOLUTION OF MONEY

Money, as we have already mentioned, is essential, or nearly so, to any advanced civilization; but anthropologists also have found some form of money in use in most of the "primitive" societies they have studied. An immense variety of things have been used for money at one time or another—shells, feathers, sharks' teeth, tobacco, and all sorts of other things. Where available, gold, silver, and copper have been most widely used as money, even long before the invention of coinage. The first coins are supposed to have been struck around 700 B.C., but gold and silver were in use by the Babylonians as early as 2000 B.C.

When we say that Yap islanders use stones for money, we obviously have in mind some test by which we can tell whether something is or is not being used for money—in other words, a definition of money. The usual definition states that money is anything that is generally acceptable in exchange for goods and services and for payment of debts. It may be worthwhile to sharpen that definition somewhat to distinguish money from any commonly used commodity. We can do that by adding that money is something that people are willing to accept in exchanges, even if they have no use for the thing themselves. In other words, money is something people accept in exchange for goods, in the expectation of passing it on to someone else in a further exchange. An essential characteristic of money is general confidence in its acceptability as a medium of exchange.

What Can Serve As Money?

Is there any reason why a community should use one thing rather than another for money? It is apparent from a glance at the list of examples of things which have served as money that the choice is not narrowly restricted. Nonetheless, there is a certain logic behind whatever thing is chosen. Until recently, most of the things used as money have had a certain intrinsic value. They have had some use for purposes other than money. Very frequently they were valued for personal ornamentation before they were used as money. In addition, they have generally had certain other properties which made them convenient to use as money. They were durable—i.e., did not deteriorate with time or wear out quickly when handled. They had a relatively high value per unit of weight so that they could be carried easily and were divisible into fairly small units. Gold, silver, and copper possessed all these properties to a greater degree than most other commodities, which is probably why they were used as money in so many places for so long.

The historical origin of the general acceptability of a particular thing in a particular area may lie in its intrinsic usefulness or the usefulness it once had. But once a thing is established in use as money, its acceptability comes to depend simply on everyone's belief that everyone else will accept it. Long before the advent of paper money, there were many cases of societies with money which no one wanted for anything except to use in exchanges. The Yap islanders, as we mentioned, use special kinds of stones as money. These stones serve no ornamental or any other purpose. Some of them are too large to move, but everyone knows who owns them. Indeed, one of them retained its value and was still used after it had fallen off a cliff into the sea.

There are all sorts of examples of useless monies, though in most cases the objects used as money were once useful or were originally tokens of some useful object. The acceptability of money does not rest on its usefulness, but rather on confidence in its continued acceptability. Money is as money does.

Many people think that the dollar is valuable because of its now somewhat tenuous connection with gold. But ask yourself what would happen to the value of gold if the U.S. Treasury refused to give $35 for every ounce of gold offered to it.

Kinds of Money in the U.S.

There are three major types of money used in the United States today—coins, paper money, and checking deposits.

Until about 300 years ago metal coins were the only kind of money in use. But in the United States, and almost everywhere else today, coins are only small change—far less important than paper currency and bank checking accounts. In the U.S. in 1963 there were $2.5 billion worth of coins in use, compared with $27 billion worth of paper money in circulation and bank checking accounts amounting to $115 billion.

The value of the metal in our coins is deliberately kept below the nominal value of the coins so that it won't be profitable to melt them down for their metallic content (as has happened in the past). The U.S. mint is always ready to supply coins in exchange for other kinds of money, and it will reverse the exchange whenever banks bring in surpluses of coin. The amount of coin in circulation, then, is just what the public wants it to be.

Most of our paper money consists of Federal Reserve Notes issued by the 12 Federal Reserve Banks. In addition to Federal Reserve Notes, a small amount of the paper money in circulation consists of "fossils"—paper money issued for one reason or another in the past. These include U.S. Notes (the Civil War "greenbacks"), Treasury Notes of 1890, Federal Reserve Bank Notes, as distinguished from Federal Reserve Notes, and National Bank Notes. The long-familiar one-dollar silver certificates are now being replaced by Federal Reserve Notes.

The largest element in our money supply consists of deposits—i.e., checking accounts in commercial banks. Checking accounts are nothing more than bookkeeping entries in the records of banks; they are not embodied in physical form like coins and bills. But they are money as much as the coins in our pockets, because checking accounts function as money. They are generally acceptable in exchange for goods and services and for payment of debts. Indeed, the volume of payments made by check is far greater than the amount of payments made with currency and coin.

We are all familiar with bank deposits and with the use of checks. But what is a bank deposit? It is not, as we are inclined to think, a pile of coins and bills in the vaults of a bank. A bank deposit is a promise on the part of the bank to pay (in coin or bills if the customer wishes) immediately on request (on demand) of the customer who owns the deposit. It is a liability of the bank. The bank owes the owner of a bank deposit and will pay him in Federal Reserve Notes or with a check on another bank if he wishes.

Of course, banks do have coins and bills in their vaults, but the amount they hold is only about 2 per cent of the deposit liabilities of banks. The vault cash held by a bank is an asset of the bank along with its other assets—government bonds, mortgages, and the IOU's of business firms to whom it has extended loans.

TABLE 1 (A)

Money Supply in the United States,
December 28, 1962 (Millions of dollars)

Silver dollars	$ 385
Other coin	2,397
Silver certificates	1,986
U.S. Notes	315
Other (In process of retirement)	172
Total Treasury currency and coin	5,255
Federal Reserve Notes	30,084
Total currency and coin	35,339
Less currency and coin in banks	4,434
Currency and coin held by the public	30,905
Demand deposits (checking accounts)	122,258
Total money supply	$153,163

TABLE 1 (B)

Supply of Near Money in the United States,
December, 1962 (Millions of dollars)

Time and savings deposits (commercial banks)	$ 97,440
Deposits at mutual savings banks	41,336
Savings-and-loan shares	80,422
U.S. Savings Bonds	46,900
U.S. securities (Due in less than 1 year)	65,972
Total	$332,070

Source: *Federal Reserve Bulletin;* 1962.

Near Monies

We consider demand deposits to be money because they can be used to pay for goods and services by means of checks. Commercial banks have other deposit liabilities called time deposits or savings deposits which differ from demand deposits only in the fact that they cannot be transferred by check. If you have a savings account and want to buy something, you have to present your pass book at your bank, withdraw currency, and then pay cash for what you buy. You cannot pay for anything with a savings deposit.

The same thing holds true for deposits in savings banks and savings-and-loan shares. Nonetheless, time and savings deposits in commercial banks, deposits in mutual savings banks, and savings-and-loan shares are regarded by their holders as almost the same thing as money, because they can be quickly and cheaply changed for money. The claims just mentioned, along with some others such as short-term U.S. Treasury securities and U.S. Savings Bonds, are frequently called "near monies" or "money substitutes."

The Evolution of Money

Our money supply consists mainly of paper money, issued by Federal Reserve Banks, and checking accounts (also called demand deposits) at banks. The Federal Reserve System controls the issue of its own notes and it indirectly controls the amount of demand deposits. Thus the amount of money in existence is controlled by a public agency.

Our present monetary system and our arrangements for controlling it reflect 300 years of experience with a variety of monetary arrangements. You will get a clearer understanding of our present system if you think of it as the product of a gradual evolution based on that experience. In the remainder of this chapter we will review some of the major steps in that evolutionary process.

THE UNRELIABILITY OF METALLIC MONEY

Faced with the problems of inflation and deflation and with constant controversy over monetary policy, some people are inclined to demand a return to the "good old days" of a monetary system based on gold coin. But the "golden age of gold coin," like other golden ages, is mythical. As we shall see, metal-coin standards often proved unsatisfactory. So did privately issued bank notes. The present system is far from perfect, but no one has thus far found a better one.

We are inclined to think that monetary problems are something relatively new. But there are frequent references to monetary problems in ancient writings. The opportunity to get something for nothing by alloying supposedly pure gold and silver coins with cheaper metals appears to have been irresistible. The debasement of coinage began almost as soon as coins were invented. The story of coinage in the ancient world is quickly revealed by Table 2, which shows changes in the Roman coinage.

TABLE 2

The Silver Content of Rome's Currency

Reign Began (A.D.)	Emperor	Per Cent Silver
98	Trajan	93
117	Hadrian	87
138	Antoninus Pius	75
161	Marcus Aurelius	68
193	Septimius Severus	50
218	Elagabalus	43
235	Maximinus	35
238	Gordian	28
244	Philip	0.5
268	Claudius Victorinus	0.02

Source: Business Review, Federal Reserve Bank of Philadelphia, January, 1960.

In western European monarchies, the story was much the same. Henry VIII was known as "old coppernose," because the silver on his coins wore off quickly, revealing the copper below. And while governments systematically debased the coinage, free enterprise did its bit. People clipped coins or shook them up in bags to collect the abraded gold scrapings.

When monarchs made two coins out of one by mixing precious metals with base metals, they did it to finance their expenditures—to fight wars or build monuments. Currency debasement led to rising prices, not because the coins contained less gold but because more of them were struck and they were spent for goods and services. Prices had to rise because expenditures rose faster than the potential output of the economy.

Coinage debasement wasn't the only cause of inflation. There was widespread inflation in Europe during the sixteenth century after the discovery of gold and silver mines in the Spanish possessions in America. Again prices went up because more coins were struck and they were spent rapidly.

Metallic coinages were seldom satisfactory, because the supply of money depended on the whims of monarchs and chance discoveries of mines. Coinage problems became unimportant only when paper money and bank deposits became the common form of money.

THE DEVELOPMENT OF BANK-NOTE MONEY

The money in use today is the product of an evolutionary process which took hundreds of years. Like so many social institutions, our monetary system is as it is because people found a way to solve certain problems in a bygone age and then adapted the solution to other problems. That's why we have to go back to the Middle Ages to understand today's monetary system.

When the Roman Empire collapsed, the highly developed monetary systems of the ancient world collapsed with it. Subsistence agriculture and petty barter dominated the scene. Money was used only in the trickle of long-distance trade in luxuries which survived.

As trade revived money became important again, and the development of new monetary systems was strongly influenced by the conditions of trade. For a long period during the Middle Ages the major economic activity involving the transfer of large sums of money was long-distance trade. Because transport was expensive and uncertain, wide price differences existed between areas producing different products. Long-distance trade was profitable, but anyone who carried a large sum of coin on a long journey ran a considerable risk of losing it to robbers or pirates. Even in towns there was considerable danger of robbery.

At the same time, the rising volume of economic activity made many people eager to borrow and willing to pay high rates of interest. Merchants wanted to borrow to buy goods to sell abroad. Nobles rich in land but poor in money were able to borrow against their rents once feudal services were commuted into money rents. Monarchs were eager to borrow to finance their wars.

These conditions provided the basis for the development of modern money and banking systems. To avoid carrying money long distances, merchants worked out arrangements for canceling debts. At the medieval fairs, merchants worked out clearing arrangements. Merchants from different places had sold goods at the fair and bought others. Instead of settling each transaction in coin, each merchant paid into a common pool the excess of the amount he bought over the amount he sold, or received from it the excess of his sales over his purchases. This arrangement reduced the amount of coin that had to be carried to and from the fair.

The same technique was then applied at a distance. An Italian merchant, shipping goods to England, would sell his claim against the English buyer to another Italian merchant who had arranged to buy in England. The Italian buying in England was then able to pay his supplier by sending him the IOU of another Englishman. The English buyer would then pay the English seller. Coin moved from one Englishman to another and from one Italian to another, but no coin had to be moved between the countries. The claims involved were represented by bills of exchange—orders by the seller to the buyer to pay the bearer the amount due. These were something like bank checks except that they were drawn by one private individual on another. After a time, bills of exchange drawn on well-known and reliable merchants were passed from hand to hand to make several different payments. This was very similar to the case in which a check on a bank is passed from hand to hand and acquires several endorsements before it is presented to the bank.

At the same time, a number of people began to act as intermediaries in the financing of loans, accepting coin from individuals with surpluses, and lending to others. The people involved in this business had varied backgrounds. Some were merchants who got into the business of borrowing and relending as a side line; some began buying and selling bills of exchange; some were lawyers who arranged the legal details of loan transactions; some were goldsmiths who became connected with finance by arranging gold shipments and weighing, assaying, and storing coin.

As early as the thirteenth century, Italian banks had begun accepting money and agreeing to repay it on demand. They lent out most of these deposits, relying on new deposits to offset the withdrawal of old ones. They kept on hand only a relatively small reserve to guard against withdrawals temporarily exceeding new deposits. They paid interest on their deposit accounts and their customers fully understood that the bank had lent out most of the coin it received. Many banks were willing to take gold, jewels, silverplate, and other valuables for safe keeping, but charged a fee for this service. Customers clearly understood the difference between warehousing coin and accepting deposits repayable at any time for the purpose of lending out the amounts received.

For a long time legal problems prevented the use of checks, but Italian banks were prepared to transfer ownership of deposits from one person to another through bookkeeping entries. But both parties to the transaction had to appear in person.

In England, goldsmiths became predominant in the banking business, and it was the English goldsmiths who led the way in the development of bank-note currency. The English goldsmiths accepted deposits—with a promise to pay on demand—and then lent most of what they received. They gave interest-bearing receipts and permitted the holders to transfer ownership of deposits by endorsing them. Presently, to make endorsements unnecessary, the receipts were made to bearer. Then because it was so convenient to make payments by giving goldsmiths' receipts, customers became willing to take non-interest-bearing receipts. As a final step, the receipts were issued in round numbers and engraved on standard forms. These were bank notes, the earliest form of paper money.

A customer taking gold coin to a goldsmith bank had two choices. He could accept bank notes in exchange for the coin, which obligated the goldsmith bank to give coin to anyone who brought the notes in for redemption. Or, he could have the bank carry a "running cash" account for him on its books. This also gave him the right to claim coin immediately on request.

A little later, legal difficulties were overcome and it became possible to transfer ownership of deposits by check. Early bank checks were simply informal notes from a depositor to his banker instructing the bank to pay a certain amount to the person named in the check.

Although early bankers accepted deposits, the use of bank notes developed much more rapidly than the use of checks. As soon as the acceptability of bank-note currency was established, note-issuing banks sprang up all over England. Many of these banks did no deposit business at all. The organizers of the bank put up a certain amount of capital in coin. They then printed notes—promises to pay coin on demand. They lent the notes to business firms and made a profit by charging interest. Thus the balance sheet of a note-issuing bank at the time of organization would look like this:

Assets		Liabilities	
Loans	$50,000	Notes outstanding	$50,000
Coin	$10,000	Capital	$10,000

In effect, the bank had exchanged its promises to pay for those of the business firms to whom it lent. It was able to collect interest on this exchange because it was prepared to meet its promises to pay on demand. The banker "created" money but he did not create wealth.

The fact that debts circulate as money and that banks do create money seems at least as odd as the use of sharks' teeth for money among primitive peoples. But the development of bank-note currency was the culmination of several hundred years of experience with the use of various kinds of evidences of debt to avoid the risks and inconvenience of carrying and storing coin. It was also a response to the generally poor state of the coinage and the willingness of businesses and government to pay high enough interest rates to make banking a worthwhile occupation.

The Problem of Reserves

Every note-issuing bank was faced with the problem of determining how many notes it could safely issue in relation to the gold reserves contributed by the partners. A bank could increase the return on its capital if it could increase its note issues and loans without raising more capital. Obviously, every bank wanted to keep as high a ratio of notes outstanding to gold reserves (or as low a ratio of reserves to notes) as possible. At the same time, it had to maintain large enough reserves to meet all requests to pay out gold in exchange for its notes. In ordinary circumstances a relatively small reserve sufficed. Notes would be returned to a bank by customers wanting coin to make wage payments (since notes were issued only in large denominations) or to make payments abroad, or they might be returned by other banks. But the bank would also receive payment for some of its loans in gold or notes of other banks which could be exchanged for gold. Ordinarily, these inflows and outflows would roughly cancel. A gold reserve was needed only to balance off the difference between daily inflows and outflows. For that purpose a reserve of only a small percentage of outstanding notes would suffice.

But should there be any doubts about a bank's liquidity or ability to meet claims against it, even a very large reserve in relation to notes outstanding might not suffice. A rumor that a bank had lent to merchants involved in an unsuccessful speculation or a hint of any kind of mismanagement could start a run on a bank. Other banks and merchants would hurry to present the bank's notes for payment in gold before it was too late. Their action would frighten others and the bank's holdings of gold would quickly be used up. A solvent bank might be able to borrow from others to meet the crisis, but whether it could get enough help quickly enough was always a question. A banker's life was anything but peaceful.

A bank which was unable to meet a run had to "stop payment"—i.e., announce its inability to give coin for its notes. The note-holders did not necessarily lose directly because of this action. The bank might ultimately collect all its loans and pay off its notes. But meanwhile its failure might involve others. Holders of the bank's notes were unable to use them to pay their debts and sometimes went bankrupt. Runs might start on other banks whose customers had gone bankrupt, or merely because the failure of one bank raised fears about the status of others. Throughout the nineteenth century English and American commercial life was upset every few years by commercial crises marked by bank and business failures.

In spite of these vicissitudes, bank notes did come into widespread use as a medium of exchange. They were not entirely satisfactory but no alternative monetary system was perfectly satisfactory either. As we have already seen, the use of gold coin did not prevent a needy government from debasing the currency, and early experiments with government issues of paper money were not very successful. Moreover, although there was some risk of loss in accepting bank notes in exchange for goods, the risk on any one transaction was small. Finally, although bank failures continued to be a problem, banking practices did improve with the passage of time.

Inconvertible Paper Money

As a result of this evolutionary process, bank notes, which were promises to pay gold coin on demand, came to be generally accepted in exchange for goods and services and for payment of debts. *In other words, they became money.*

Originally, bank notes were simply promises to pay money—no different from any other IOU's. Most promises to pay are not generally acceptable in exchange for goods and services because (1) they do not promise immediate payment; (2) the ability and willingness of the issuer (debtor) is subject to question; (3) certain legal formalities are necessary to transfer ownership of the claim.

Early bankers were able to establish the general acceptability of their notes by (1) achieving almost unquestioned credit standing by meeting their obligations without fail over a long period; and (2) creating a form of IOU which was payable on demand, readily identifiable, and transferable without legal formalities.

At first, bank notes were regarded as claims which served as useful *substitutes for money, but only gold and silver coin was regarded as real money.* With the passage of time, however, people ceased to draw any distinction between the real thing and the substitute. Bank notes were just as readily acceptable in trading transactions as gold coin, so they were just as much money as was gold coin. Nonetheless, bank notes still had to meet the test of redemption for gold coin. People who needed coin to make payments in foreign countries, or for some other special purpose, or who simply distrusted banks, had the right to ask the banker for gold coin in exchange for his notes. If the banker failed to deliver, everyone else presented his notes and the bank had to close. But though bank money had to meet the redemption test, it was clearly money because it was generally acceptable as a medium of exchange.

The final step in this evolution was reached when people became so used to bank notes that they were prepared to accept notes which could not be converted into gold. The notes of the Bank of England and the Federal Reserve are formal liabilities of a bank—promises to pay something. But neither institution will in fact convert its notes into anything else. Foreign central banks can exchange dollars for gold but no one else can do so. People became willing to accept them after convertibility into gold ceased because everyone was confident that everyone else would accept them. And they felt confident because everyone had in fact accepted them for a long time. The notes originally became generally acceptable in exchange because they were convertible into gold. But once sufficient confidence in their acceptability had been built up, the convertibility prop to confidence could be removed like a temporary scaffolding.

Deposit Banking

Use of bank notes in England was established by the end of the seventeenth century and very widespread by the middle of the eighteenth century. Deposit banking and the use of checks to transfer ownership of deposits developed much more slowly. But by the end of the eighteenth century the use of checks was very common, particularly among London merchants and financial houses. A number of banks which accepted deposits subject to check but did not issue notes had been organized in London.[1]

As the volume of trade grew with the progress of the commercial and industrial revolutions, merchants found it increasingly convenient to use checks instead of bank notes. The large merchants in London began to bring gold coin and bank notes into the London deposit banks and to pay by check. Since the total volume of trade was rising rapidly, the volume of bank notes in circulation also continued to rise.

At first glance, a demand deposit may not seem to be much like a bank note, but in two fundamental respects they are the same: (1) demand deposits, like bank notes, are liabilities of banks (promises to pay standard money on demand); (2) both are used as a means of payment for goods and services.

The difference lies in the way in which they circulate. Bank notes circulate from hand to hand and can be used many times without ever appearing at a bank. On the other hand, demand deposits circulate by check and most of the checks drawn on the deposits of one bank will be deposited at another. The receiving bank then has a claim on the bank on which the check was drawn. Every day every bank receives checks on other banks and it is necessary for banks to settle their claims on one another. The method of settlement is called clearing checks.

If there are two banks in the community, each bank will receive checks on the other each day. On a particular day bank *A* may receive in deposits $10,000 worth of checks drawn on *B* while *B* receives $12,000 worth of checks on *A*. Representatives of the two banks meet each day and exchange the checks received. *A* owes *B* $2,000 which must be paid in notes or coin. Notice that only $2,000 of notes and coin have to move in order to carry out $22,000 worth of transactions.

We have pointed out the similarities between bank notes and demand

---

[1] This development was speeded up when the Bank of England was granted a monopoly of note issue in the London area.

deposits—both are demand claims against a bank and both can "circulate" as means of payment. There is another similarity. Demand deposits, like bank notes, are *fractional reserve money*. If you looked at the books of one of the London deposit banks, you would find that they did not appear very different from those of a note-issuing bank. The statement might look something like this:

Assets

Loans	$80,000	Capital stock	$ 10,000
Currency and coin	$30,000	Demand deposits	$100,000

The bank has deposits of several times its "reserve" of currency and coin, just as a note-issuing bank has notes outstanding to a value which is several times as great as its reserve. In fact, banks create deposits just as they manufacture bank notes.

How Banks Create Money

The balance sheet of a deposit bank resembles that of a note-issuing bank. But there is an important difference in the way in which banks create deposits. A note-issuing bank started with a certain amount of capital and lent an amount of notes representing several times as much. A deposit bank began in a different way. It obtained some initial funds from customers who brought in currency and coin and took a deposit credit on the bank's books (against which checks could be written) in exchange.

Deposit banking is based on the principle that all the customers who have brought funds to the bank will not withdraw them at once. On any day some of the customers will withdraw funds in cash or by checks presented by other banks at the clearinghouse. But other customers will increase their deposits by bringing in cash or checks on other banks.

Experience shows that in normal circumstances deposits and withdrawals tend to balance. A bank needs a cash reserve because deposits and withdrawals do not balance exactly. Banks have generally found that reserves of less than 20 per cent of deposits are adequate to meet occasional excesses of withdrawals over deposits.

Deposit Expansion Stage 1

A bank, having received some cash from customers who have brought funds to the bank, is therefore in a position to make loans or investments. A bank, say bank *A,* starting out with deposits in currency and coin of $100,000, might feel safe to lend $80,000. In a check-using community, the bank would make its loans by giving the borrowers the right to draw checks against it. The right to draw checks is called a demand deposit even though the borrower hasn't deposited anything. (If you like, you may consider that the bank gives currency to the borrower when it makes the loan and that he then deposits it in the bank.) These transactions are summarized below:

1. Customers exchange coin and bank notes for the right to draw checks. These changes would appear in the bank's balance sheet:

Bank A

Assets	Liabilities
Notes and Coins + $100,000	Customers' Deposits + $100,000

2. The bank needs a reserve of notes and coin equal only to 20 per cent of deposit claims. It lends an amount equal to its "excess" reserve. It makes the loan by giving the borrowers deposit credit and receiving their promissory notes in exchange. These changes would appear in the bank's balance sheet:

Bank A

Assets	Liabilities
Promissory Notes + 80,000	Borrowers' Deposits + 80,000

3. Add the changes in steps 1 and 2.

Bank A

Assets		Liabilities	
Notes and Coin	+ 100,000	Customers' Deposits	+ 100,000
Promissory Notes	+ 80,000	Borrowers' Deposits	+ 80,000
	180,000		180,000

Of course, the borrowers will spend the proceeds of the loans very quickly. Otherwise they would not have borrowed. They will write checks or withdraw currency. Then the bank will lose a corresponding amount of its reserve in currency and coin. Therefore, the bank can afford to lend only *an amount equal to the excess of currency and coin over the amount it requires as reserves.*

Our deposit bank has manufactured money. After the bank has made its loans, there is $80,000 more of money in existence than there was before. The deposit claims of the original depositors are money, since the holders expect to use them to buy things. And the borrowers also have money either in currency or in the deposit claims they were given when they borrowed. When they spend it, the money doesn't disappear—someone else receives it. So although the mechanics are somewhat different, banks which accept demand deposits subject to check, manufacture money just as note-issuing banks do. The acceptability of the deposit claims against banks, of course, rests on confidence in banks, just as in the case of bank notes. Once bank notes paved the way, it was much easier for people to get used to exchanging bank deposits than it was for them to get used to using bank notes.

Multiple Expansion of Deposits

Now let us examine one other point about the operations of deposit banks. We mentioned that the proceeds of deposit claims arising from loan transactions would be quickly withdrawn. If they were withdrawn in cash and the cash remained in circulation, that would be the end of the story. But suppose the borrowers drew checks against their accounts and the recipients deposited the checks in another bank, *B*. The bank receiving the checks would present them at the clearinghouse and (leaving other transactions aside) would collect currency and coin from the first bank. A summary of these transactions follows:

4. The borrowers draw checks on bank *A* which are received by customers of bank *B*. Bank *A* pays the other bank in gold and bank notes. Changes in the banks' balance sheets are shown below:

Bank A

Assets	Liabilities
Notes and Coin — 80,000	Deposits — 80,000

Bank B

Assets	Liabilities
Notes and Coin + 80,000	Deposits + 80,000

5. Adding the changes in (4) to those in (3), the net changes in bank *A*'s balance sheet now look like this:

Bank A

Assets		Liabilities	
Notes and Coins	+ 20,000	Deposits	+ 100,000
Promissory Notes	+ 80,000		

Notice that bank *A* has a reserve equal to 20 per cent of its deposits. Its balance sheet looks very much like that of a note-issuing bank. But as we have seen, it arrived at that position by an entirely different route. It didn't create an amount of money equal to five times its initial deposit. It created an amount of money equal to four-fifths of its initial deposit. Then all the new deposits were withdrawn and it lost four-fifths of the reserves obtained from the initial deposit. It was then left with a reserve equal to one-fifth of the initial deposit.

Deposit Expansion Stage 2

Bank *B* would have no reason to distinguish these deposits from any others and would therefore have more reserves than it needed. Having acquired $80,000 in coin against new deposits of the same amount, it needs a reserve of $16,000 and has excess reserves of $64,000. It is therefore in a position to make loans of $64,000. The borrowers will be given deposit credit for $64,000 but may be expected to withdraw it in cash or by check very shortly. When they have done so, bank *B* will be left with $16,000 in coin and deposit liabilities of $80,000—a 20 per cent ratio of reserves to deposits. Bank *B* has now created another $64,000, since the depositors of the $80,000 regard their claims as money and someone else has $64,000 in coin. The two banks together have therefore created $144,000. (Total deposits have increased by $180,000, and $64,000 is still in circulation, making a total of $244,000 from the original deposit of $100,000.) The transactions just described are summarized below:

6. Bank *B* is now in the same position as bank *A* after step 1. It needs a reserve of only 20 per cent against the $80,000 of deposits received from checks on *A*. It needs a reserve of $16,000 and has excess reserves of $64,000. To increase earnings it lends an equal amount.

Bank B

Assets		Liabilities	
Loans	+ 64,000	Deposits	+ 64,000

The borrowers will write checks on *B* which will be deposited in another bank, *C*. *B* pays *C* with notes and coin.

Bank B

Assets		Liabilities	
Notes and Coins	— 64,000	Deposits	— 64,000

Bank C

Assets		Liabilities	
Notes and Coins	+ 64,000	Deposits	+ 64,000

As in the case of bank A, the withdrawals from deposits created by bank *B*'s loans might be withdrawn in cash or by check. Suppose they are all withdrawn by check and the checks are deposited in a third bank, *C*. Then the whole process could be repeated with bank *C* "creating" another chunk of money 80 per cent as large as its predecessor. Obviously, the process could go on indefinitely, with the amount of money created at each step getting smaller and smaller.

Ultimately, the whole set of banks could create an amount of money (in the form of deposits) equal to several times the amount of the original deposit. How much would depend on the size of the reserve in coin they felt it necessary to hold, and on the proportion of the proceeds of their loans taken in cash instead of in checks deposited in other banks.

Deposit banks thus create money just as note-issuing banks do. The attitude of the public toward bank deposits changed gradually in the same way as its attitude toward bank notes. At first, checking deposits were regarded as only a substitute for real money—first coin then bank notes. Some people still feel that way. But with the passage of time the use of checks became more widespread and nowadays far more payments are made by check than by currency. If money is a medium of exchange, then checking deposits are certainly money. A more complete discussion of the deposit expansion process under modern conditions can be found in Chapter 3.

Public Control of the Money Supply

There is one difference between the historical development of the use of bank notes and of bank deposits. The issue of bank notes was eventually taken over by government controlled institutions and the notes ceased to be convertible into gold coin. The "issue" of bank deposits has remained in private hands. And a private bank must still be prepared to convert deposits into currency on demand.

The development of private banks which issued notes and generated deposits placed control of the money supply in private hands. The minting of coins remained a prerogative of government, but the ancient trick of coinage debasement seemed petty when compared with the power of the private banking system. In England, where banking developed most rapidly, a needy government resorted to the banking system instead of attempting to manipulate the coinage. Indeed, the Bank of England was founded in an effort to finance the government. The bank was granted a monopoly of note issue in the London area in return for a large loan to the government.

By the end of the eighteenth century it was widely believed that the money supply, like everything else, would be automatically regulated by private competition, provided the government kept its hands off. But, as we have already pointed out, individual banks had great difficulty in managing their affairs and bank failures were frequent in England and America throughout the nineteenth century. The total money supply also moved erratically, sometimes increasing rapidly, sometimes declining abruptly. The record of private competition in regulating the money supply was as unsatisfactory as that of royal control. In England the Bank of England acquired the power and took the responsibility of controlling the money supply and thus solved many, though by no means all, of the problems of a privately controlled money supply. American monetary history followed a different path, although ultimately a central bank was created to control the money supply.

Summary

Many different things have been used as money at one time or another. Some of them have been useful objects but others were merely tokens. Anything can serve as money so long as everyone is confident of its acceptability in exchange for goods and services. It does not matter whether that confidence originates in law, custom, or in the intrinsic value of the objects used as money.

Our money consists mainly of demand deposits—checking accounts— and Federal Reserve notes, and of relatively small amounts of coin and other kinds of paper money.

Our present monetary system is the result of hundreds of years of evolution in the use of money. Merchants exchanged promises to pay in order to avoid the use of coin. The use of bank notes gradually developed out of that experience. Later another kind of claim against banks—the demand deposit—came into widespread use. Bank deposits can be used as money because ownership of deposits can be transferred by the use of checks.

Nowadays bank notes are issued by government-sponsored institutions like the Federal Reserve Bank and the Bank of England. But demand deposits are still issued or created by private banks.

Note-issuing banks were able to issue an amount of notes equal to several times the amount of their reserves in coin. They were able to do so because only a fraction of those receiving the bank notes wanted to redeem them in coin.

Deposit banks also have deposit liabilities equal to several times the amount of their reserves. But the process by which banks "create" deposits equal to several times the amount of their reserves and coin is more complicated than the note-issue process.

3

THE DEVELOPMENT OF MONEY
AND BANKING IN THE UNITED STATES

Before the Revolution, the American colonies got along with a rather make-shift monetary system. English and foreign coins—often clipped and abraded —circulated simultaneously. The colonies frequently issued paper money as a means of covering their expenses without resort to taxation—even with representation. With equal frequency, amounts issued grew until the paper money depreciated in terms of gold and silver coin and in terms of goods. The English government finally prohibited the colonial governments from issuing paper money.

During the Revolution the Continental Congress issued large amounts of paper dollars to pay for the war, such large amounts relative to the resources of the country that "continentals" eventually became a synonym for worthlessness. They were eventually redeemed at $.01 on the dollar. After the adoption of the Constitution, the federal government began to mint gold and silver coins. The Treasury issued paper money during the War of 1812 but that issue was redeemed for gold shortly afterward. Until the Civil War there were no further issues of paper money by the Treasury, except for a minor one during the Mexican War.

Although the federal government refrained from issuing paper money, banks entered the field enthusiastically. Every state chartered banks and subjected them to whatever regulation it saw fit—which was often very little. Checks still were not widely used. Banks made their profits by lending their own notes, which were then put into circulation by the borrowers. The reserve for redemption of the notes in coin was provided by the capital subscribed by the proprietors. The bank which could keep the largest number of notes in circulation per dollar of reserve earned the highest return on capital. Many banks maintained adequate reserves and were able to redeem all the notes returned for coin. But others, particularly in some of the western and southern states, issued notes with little concern for the problem of redemption.

In 1861 a writer in the *Chicago Tribune* said the "bank nuisance has become unbearable." According to that writer many banks made it their chief business to manufacture and put out as large an amount as they could by any contrivance keep in circulation, regardless of the dearth of reserves. Some were "merely banks of circulation without capital and doing no business at their nominal locations," the notes being issued at goodly distances from the place of redemption so as to delay presentation. Many main offices where redemptions were made "were located in the depths of forests where there were few human inhabitations, but plenty of wildcats. Thus they came to be known as the wildcat banks." Most of the Chicago banks issued notes through agent banks in Georgia. In addition to the factor of risk, bank notes sank in value in proportion to distance and other difficulties in presenting them for redemption. The same objective of delaying presentation for redemption was accomplished by the issue of "post notes," payable 30 or 60 days after date.

From the Revolution until the Civil War the commercial life of the U.S. was constantly plagued with the problems posed by the circulation of counterfeit bank notes, or bank notes issued by closed or non-existent banks. Notes passed at discounts which varied with the distance from the issuing point and the reputation of banks in the state from which they came.

This situation persisted for two reasons. In the expanding western areas there was an intense demand for credit. Farmers and others who wanted to invest in land, buildings, and equipment resisted attempts to regulate banking because they feared that their access to bank credit would be limited by regulation. Second, given the existence of a bank currency, every seller of goods was constantly faced with a choice between selling his goods for bank notes or losing the sale (or taking a lower price) if he insisted on payment in coin. Each seller was willing to take some risk in accepting bank notes in the expectation of passing them on to someone else.

In the pre-Civil War period, two abortive attempts to provide some central control of banking was made. The first bank of the United States operated from 1797 to 1810 and the Second Bank of the United States from 1816 to 1836. These banks were chartered by the federal government and had a much larger initial capital than other banks. They were depositories for federal government funds. Though they were private banks, they attempted to exercise some control over private bank-note issues by promptly returning for redemption in gold all the notes of other banks which they received. In that way a bank which issued too large an amount of notes in relation to its reserves of coin was soon drained of reserves and failed.

This check to the expansion of bank credit was resented in the expanding western sections of the country, and neither bank was able to get its charter renewed by Congress. From 1836 until the Civil War there were constant demands for Congress to do something about the state of the currency, but no action was taken until it was forced by the Civil War.

During the Civil War the federal government printed paper money— "greenbacks"—to finance the war. In addition, the government authorized the chartering of national banks which were given the privilege of issuing notes secured by U.S. bonds. At the same time, a tax was levied on notes issued by state-chartered banks, which made their note issues unprofitable. Most of the state-chartered banks took out new charters as national banks. For the first time, the U.S. had a banking system which was subject to a uniform set of regulations and a currency which was directly regulated by the federal government.

GROWTH OF DEPOSIT BANKING

Just when the currency problem seemed to be solved, the importance of note issues in the total money supply began to decline. The use of checks to transfer ownership of bank deposits began at about the same time as bank-note issues. But the use of checks developed much more slowly than the use of bank notes. After the Civil War, however, the rapid industrialization of the United States led to an equally rapid increase in the volume of payments to be made. Bank notes serve well enough for small-scale payments between individuals in direct contact with one another. But payment by check is obviously much more convenient for business firms engaged in large-scale transactions. Before the Civil War, it had been considered impossible to operate a bank profitably without the bank-note privilege. But within a few years after the Civil War a large number of state-chartered banks specializing only in deposit banking were organized.

Defects of the National Banking System

The national banking system was a great improvement over the pre-Civil War system but was very inadequate for a country which was coming of age as a great industrial nation. The period between the Civil War and the First World War was one of great industrial expansion. But this spectacular growth was periodically interrupted by financial panics and depression. In 1878, 1883, and 1907 there were waves of bank failures, stock prices collapsed, thousands of business firms failed. These panics were followed by depressions marked by low industrial production and high unemployment. Many factors helped to produce these episodes of panic and depression, but everyone agreed that the weaknesses of the banking system were partly responsible and certainly intensified depressions after they began.

The national banking system effectively prevented the overissue of notes by wildcat banks, but it went too far in the other direction. An expanding country needs an increasing amount of currency for hand-to-hand transactions, and it needs more at some seasons of the year than at others. The national banking system provided a uniform currency but made no provision for varying the amount with the needs of the country. Every fall, businesses would withdraw in currency from banks to pay farmers for crops. Banks would have to pay out their reserves. There were thousands of banks, many of them very small and many badly managed. Some banks always found themselves without enough reserves to meet currency withdrawals and had to close. The banks might be solvent but could not quickly convert their loans into cash.

The problem was compounded by the fact that small-town banks were allowed to keep part of their reserves on deposit with large city banks. When country banks needed currency, they drew on those deposits. The city banks then had to find the necessary currency quickly. In most years the banking system managed to stagger through the fall season with only a modest number of bank failures. But periodically some event—a decline in stock prices, or the failure of an important business firm—would raise fears about the solvency of banks. People would then try to convert deposits into currency and that demand, on top of the seasonal demand, would be too much for the banking system. Some important bank would fail and that would intensify the public's fears. Every bank would be subjected to heavy withdrawals of currency. They would all try to raise cash by selling securities and calling loans, thus depressing security prices and causing business failures. Clearly, what was needed was some device which would keep the volume of currency and deposits under control—avoid the excesses of free banking—yet permit sufficient flexibility to meet the needs of an expanding economy.

After the panic of 1907, demand for changes in the banking system became intense and a National Monetary Commission was established. It delivered a voluminous report in 1911 covering the experience of the American banking systems and of foreign systems. The recommendations of the report, though considerably revised, became the basis for the establishment of the Federal Reserve System in 1914.

The Federal Reserve System

The National Monetary Commission recommended the establishment of a central bank modeled on long-established European institutions like the Bank of England and the Bank of France. In deference to the forces of regionalism and agrarian fear of control by eastern financial centers, the Federal Reserve Act established not 1 but 12 banks. The country was divided into 12 Federal Reserve Districts each served by a Federal Reserve Bank. The banks are nominally private corporations whose stock is owned by the commercial banks they serve. In practice, the broad policy of the whole system is controlled by the Board of Governors of the Federal Reserve System, who are appointed by the president. Many decisions are left to the officers and directors of the 12 banks, so that the system provides a uniform basic monetary policy whose detailed administration can be responsive to the special needs and conditions of the different parts of the country.

All national banks were required to become members of the Federal Reserve System; state-chartered banks might become members if they wished and met certain conditions. The Federal Reserve provided for a new, centralized system for maintaining bank reserves, for a new method of issuing currency, and made it possible for individual member banks to borrow from the Federal Reserve Banks. Most important of all, the new legislation put control of the nation's money supply into the hands of the Board of Governors of the Federal Reserve System.

Under the national banking system, banks had held reserves either in currency and coin in their own vaults or in the form of deposit claims on other banks. Under the new system, member banks were required to maintain deposits at the Federal Reserve Bank in their district. These reserve deposits must be equal to a certain percentage of a bank's demand deposit liabilities and a lower percentage of time and saving deposits (see Table 3). The reserve deposit which a bank must hold is called its "required reserve." Reserve balances over and above those required by the law are referred to as "excess reserves." The Board of Governors has the power to vary the reserve requirement percentages within broad limits.

The banks which entered the system at its formation in 1914 met the reserve requirement by transferring currency and coin formerly held in their vaults to the Federal Reserve Banks, receiving deposit credit on the books of the Federal Reserve Banks.

Banks also acquired reserves as a result of gold imports to the United States. A considerable amount of foreign gold was sold in the United States during and after the First World War, and even larger amounts during the 1930's.

TABLE 3

Required Reserves, July, 1963

	Against Demand Deposits	Against Time Deposits
City Banks	16½%	4%
Country Banks	12	4

(Since 1960, member banks have been permitted to count part of their vault cash as reserves.)

FEDERAL RESERVE LENDING TO MEMBER BANKS

A member bank which finds it difficult to meet its reserve requirements may borrow from the Federal Reserve Bank in its district. In order to borrow, a member bank must deposit U.S. securities or promissory notes of business firms to which the bank has made loans. The Federal Reserve Bank extends the loans by giving the bank credit in its reserve deposit account. In effect, the Federal Reserve Bank exchanges liabilities with the member bank. The member bank owes the Federal Reserve Bank because of the loan, but the Federal Reserve Bank owes the member bank as well because the "deposit" is a claim against the Federal Reserve Bank.

The member banks that borrow from Federal Reserve Banks pay interest on their indebtedness. The rate of interest charged them is called the "discount rate." By varying this rate the Federal Reserve Bank can make it more profitable or less profitable for banks to borrow.

In addition, the Federal Reserve Banks limit the amount of member-bank borrowing by warning banks that borrow too much, too often, or for too long a time. The privilege of borrowing is very seldom refused, but without any formal action the Federal Reserve Banks make member banks aware that they are overworking the discount privilege.

NOTE ISSUE

The Federal Reserve Banks issue the bulk of our currency. Federal Reserve Notes issued in denominations of $1 to $10,000 are liabilities of the Federal Reserve Bank. They are legal tender for all debts and tax payments. In order to issue notes, a Federal Reserve Bank must deposit with the Treasury at least 25 cents in gold for every dollar of notes issued and 75 cents in government securities or suitable promissory notes of business firms.

The Federal Reserve Banks could, if they wished, put their notes into circulation by using them to buy government securities or paying them out to member banks when making loans. In practice, however, the Federal Reserve Banks issue notes to banks in much the same way as a bank pays out cash to its customers. When a member bank's customer requests currency, the bank pays it out from currency held in its vault—and, of course, charges (reduces) the deposit account of the person making the withdrawal. If the bank feels that it has insufficient currency in its vault, it requests more from its Federal Reserve Bank. The Federal Reserve Bank in turn pays out the notes and charges (reduces) the deposit account of the member bank.

This arrangement met the currency problems that had arisen under the national banking system. In the fall when business usually expands and banks have to pay out a great deal of currency, member banks obtain additional currency from Federal Reserve Banks. After the first of the year, bank customers usually deposit more currency than they take out. Member banks then return the excess currency to Federal Reserve Banks. Thus the seasonal shortage of currency which plagued the national banking system is eliimnated.

Until 1933 the status of Federal Reserve Notes was essentially the same as that of the bank notes issued by private banks. They were liabilities of the Federal Reserve Bank issuing them and were a promise to pay "lawful money"—gold coin or Treasury currency—on demand. They could be issued to a bank in the course of making loans to a bank just as private banks used to issue their notes to individual customers in the course of making loans to them. The one difference between Federal Reserve Notes and the private bank notes of the pre-Civil War period was that Federal Reserve Notes were "legal tender for all debts public and private." That expression means that anyone who offers to pay his debts or taxes in Federal Reserve Notes has discharged his obligation. Since the volume of debt is always very large, the legal-tender status of Federal Reserve Notes insures their acceptability in all kinds of transactions. After 1933 the Federal Reserve Banks were no longer obligated to pay out gold coin in exchange for their notes. But their legal-tender status, together with the fact that everyone was used to them, insured the continued acceptability of the notes.

FEDERAL RESERVE SECURITY PURCHASES

Banks gain reserves from gold imports, and when they borrow from the Federal Reserve; they lose reserves when currency in circulation increases, when gold is exported, or when member banks repay debts to Federal Reserve Banks. In discussing the national banking system, we mentioned that banking panics were caused in part at least by the difficulties faced by banks in meeting a loss of reserves due to an increased demand for currency or a loss of gold. The ability of Federal Reserve Banks to lend to member banks absorbs these disturbances. But it is not necessary for the Federal Reserve System to be passive in this matter. The Federal Reserve need not wait for banks to borrow. It can actively defend the banking system from disturbances caused by gains or losses of reserves associated with the flow of currency and gold. The Federal Reserve can provide the banking system as a whole with additional reserves by purchasing government securities from the public.

The process works out as follows: the Federal Reserve Bank orders securities from a government-bond dealer who will in turn buy them from someone else. The Federal Reserve Bank pays with a check on itself. The person selling the securities will deposit the check in a commercial bank which will (a) credit the customer's deposit account, and (b) send the check to the Federal Reserve Bank for credit in its reserve deposit account (see p. 30 for balance-sheet entries).

As a result of its purchase of securities, the Federal Reserve Bank has increased its own assets and its own liabilities, in the form of member-bank reserve balances. At the same time, member banks have increased their liabilities to customers (customer deposits) and have gained an asset in the form of an increased claim against the Federal Reserve Bank.

The Federal Reserve Bank has created additional reserve balances with the stroke of the pen, in just the same way that it can manufacture notes with a printing press.

Federal Reserve Banks could pay for securities with their own notes, but if they did so the security sellers would almost surely deposit the notes in member banks which would send them to the Federal Reserve to receive credit in their reserve deposit accounts. It saves trouble to issue checks instead of notes, but the effect is the same.

The process of increasing bank reserves by buying securities can be reversed. The Federal Reserve Banks usually buy securities in the fall months and sell them after the turn of the year when a large amount of currency returns to banks with the seasonal fall in retail sales. The sale of securities by the Federal Reserve Banks has exactly the opposite effect of a security purchase. Thus it is possible for the Federal Reserve Banks to control the volume of bank reserves at will. Federal Reserve purchases and sales of United States securities are called *open-market operations.*

The Federal Reserve System can and frequently does use its powers to buy and sell securities to keep bank reserves constant—selling securities to offset gains in reserves from other sources and buying to offset losses from other sources. But if it wishes, it can use those same powers to make a net addition to the supply of bank reserves. When it does that, the volume of bank deposits tends to expand by several times as much as the change in reserves. The ability to control bank reserves by the use of open-market operations is one of the Federal Reserve System's most important powers. The process by which the volume of bank deposits expands is essentially the same as the one outlined in Chapter 2.

Deposit Expansion under the Federal Reserve System

In Chapter 2 we showed how a deposit of coin in a commercial bank would lead to the creation of a total amount of deposits several times the amount of the original deposit. American banks still operate on the *fractional reserve* principle, and deposit expansion still occurs in the way in which it was described in Chapter 2. Nowadays, of course, banks use Federal Reserve facilities for clearing checks, but that is only a mechanical difference. And reserve requirements are not a matter of judgment for the individual banker but are set by the Board of Governors.

The most important difference between modern banking and early deposit banking is the nature of the funds which constitute bank reserves. In the banking system described in Chapter 2, banks held reserves in coin or currency. They got those reserves in the first instance when individuals or business firms brought in coin or currency which had been hoarded or used in hand-to-hand transactions or which had been imported.

The original deposits which provide banks with reserves today consist of checks on Federal Reserve Banks. Of course, people do desposit currency in banks, but they also withdraw it, and on balance the withdrawals of currency exceed the deposits.

Let us suppose that the Board of Governors decides that an expansion of the money supply is appropriate. It instructs the Federal Reserve Bank of New York to buy $1 million worth of U.S. securities. Through a bond dealer in New York, the bank buys the securities from some individual or corporation, paying with a check on itself. The seller deposits the check in some commercial bank (bank *A*). Bank *A* will credit the seller's account and return the check to the Federal Reserve Bank for credit in its reserve account.

Bank *A* has now increased its deposit liabilities by $1 million and its assets in the form of reserve deposits at the Federal Reserve Bank by the same amount. The Federal Reserve Bank has increased its deposit liabilities (member-bank reserve deposits) by $1 million and its assets, in the form of U.S. securities, by an equal amount.

The transaction has resulted in the creation of a million dollars of demand deposits and a million dollars of additional bank reserves. No one is richer because of it. The public holds a million dollars more demand deposits but it holds a million dollars less U.S. securities. This transaction and the others following it are summarized in the numbered steps below:

1. When the Federal Reserve Bank purchases government securities, a member bank gains reserves because the seller of the securities deposits the check drawn on the Federal Reserve in his bank (bank *A*) which then sends the check to its Federal Reserve Bank and receives credit in its reserve account. The changes in the balance sheet of bank *A* and the Federal Reserve Banks would be represented thus:

Federal Reserve Bank

Assets	Liabilities
U.S. Securities + 1,000,000	Member Bank Reserve Deposits Bank A + 1,000,000

Bank A

Assets	Liabilities
Reserves with Federal Reserve Bank + 1,000,000	Customer Deposits + 1,000,000

The story doesn't end there, however. Bank *A* has increased its reserves and deposits by $1 million but its *required* reserve has increased by only $150,000. It therefore gained *excess* reserves of $850,000.

Bank *A* is now in a position to expand its earning assets by making additional loans or buying securities. It can make loans or buy securities in an amount equal to its excess reserve ($850,000). We will see in a moment why it wouldn't be safe to go beyond that amount. If business is expanding, bank *A* may make additional loans of $850,000. It will make the loan by crediting the deposit account of the borrower, receiving a promissory note from the borrower in exchange. Bank *A* will have added to its deposit liabilities by $850,000 and to its assets in loans by an equal amount.

2. Additional deposits are created when a bank with excess reserves makes loans by crediting borrowers' deposit accounts for the amount of the loan. The changes in bank *A*'s balance sheet are shown below:

Bank A

Assets	Liabilities
Loans + 850,000	Borrower Deposits + 850,000

This is the first stage of deposit expansion by commercial banks. Taking the original action of the Federal Reserve together with bank *A*'s action in making loans, commercial banks and the Federal Reserve System have added $1,850,000 to demand deposits.

3. The Federal Reserve purchase, together with the loans made by bank *A*, has increased loans and deposits by a total of $1,850,000, loans by $850,000, and member bank reserves by $1,000,000. The changed position of bank *A* as a result of the two sets of transactions is shown thus:

Bank A

Assets		Liabilities	
Reserves with Federal Reserve Bank	+ 1,000,000	Initial Deposits	+ 1,000,000
Loans	+ 850,000	Stage 1 Deposits	+ 850,000
		Total	+ 1,850,000

Of course, things won't stay that way very long. The business firms who borrowed from bank *A* did so because they wanted to buy something. The borrowers wanted to buy raw materials or equipment. Once they get the loan, they will buy what they need and pay for it by check. The businesses receiving the checks *might* be customers of bank *A*, but since there are 13,000 banks in the United States, that is not very likely. The checks written by those who borrowed from bank *A* will be deposited in other banks. The other banks will send the checks to a Federal Reserve Bank for credit in their reserve accounts. The Federal Reserve Bank will charge bank *A*'s reserve account and return the checks to bank *A*. Bank *A* will, of course, charge the borrowers' account when it gets the checks.

Notice that these transactions leave the total of bank reserves unchanged but pass the reserves on from bank *A* to other banks.

4. When borrowers write checks, deposits and reserves are transferred from bank *A* to other banks. Total reserves and deposits remain unchanged. The changes in the banks balance sheets are shown below:

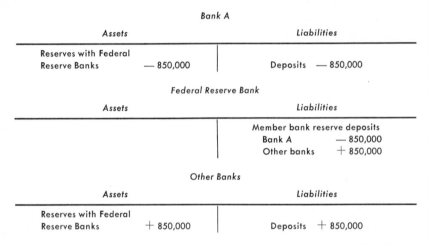

Bank A

Assets	Liabilities
Reserves with Federal Reserve Banks — 850,000	Deposits — 850,000

Federal Reserve Bank

Assets	Liabilities
	Member bank reserve deposits
	Bank A — 850,000
	Other banks + 850,000

Other Banks

Assets	Liabilities
Reserves with Federal Reserve Banks + 850,000	Deposits + 850,000

We now see why bank *A* could not expand loans by more than the $850,000 of excess reserves. The bank knew that the borrowers were going to draw checks against the deposit credit given them when the loans were made. It knew that the only safe procedure is to assume that for every dollar of deposits created by lending, a dollar of reserves will be lost to another bank.

After all these transactions, bank *A* winds up just meeting its required reserve. It has a million dollars more in deposit liabilities than it had at the start. Its reserve deposit is up by $150,000 as required by law, and it has increased its loans by $850,000. The final position of bank *A* is shown below:

Bank A

Assets	Liabilities
Reserves with Federal Reserve Bank + 150,000	Deposits + 1,000,000
Loans + 850,000	

Now notice the position of "other" banks shown in step 4. It's exactly like the position of bank *A* in step 1 except that the amounts involved in step 4 are only 85 per cent of those in step 1.

They are now ready to generate a second stage of commercial bank deposit expansion. These "other," or "stage-2," banks have excess reserves of $722,500 (85% of $850,000). They can make loans in that amount, creating an equivalent amount of deposits in the process.

5. Banks which gained reserves from bank A (step 4 above) expand loans and deposits. The bookkeeping entries resulting from those transactions are shown thus:

Stage-2 Banks

Assets	Liabilities
Loans + 722,500	Borrowers' Deposits + 722,500

6. The banking system has now generated a total of $2,572,500 in new deposits, $1,572,500 of loans. The change to date for the whole banking system is shown thus:

All Commercial Banks

Assets		Liabilities	
Reserves with Federal		Deposits	
Reserve Bank	+ 1,000,000	Initial	+ 1,000,000
Loans		Stage 1	+ 850,000
Stage 1	850,000	Stage 2	+ 722,500
Stage 2	722,500		2,572,500
Total Loans	+ 1,572,500	Total Deposits	+ 2,572,500

The stage-2 banks will lose deposits and reserves when borrowers spend the proceeds. The stage-2 banks will be left with deposits of $850,000 and reserves of $126,500, which leaves them with a reserve of just 15 per cent.

The $722,500 of deposits created by the stage-2 banks and an equivalent amount of reserves will have passed to a third group of banks. They require a reserve of $107,000 and have excess reserves of $614,500.

The whole process can then be repeated by these stage-3 banks. And, of course, when that stage is completed, the process can be repeated again. Indeed, it can go on indefinitely. But the amount of new loans and deposits generated at each step of the process becomes progressively smaller. In fact, each step is 85 per cent the size of the preceding one. The banks at each stage can create new deposits equal to 85 per cent of the reserves they gain as a result of deposit creation by banks in the preceding stage. The other 15 per cent is tied up in required reserves against the deposits transferred from other banks.

The whole process is summed up in the chart on page 34.

Banks at each stage received deposits and reserves (column 1) from other banks (in the case of bank A, as a result of the Federal Reserve Bank's action; after that, each bank receives deposits and reserves because other banks have made loans against which checks were drawn and deposited in the banks in question.) Only 15 per cent of the reserves received are required against the deposits received (column 2). The remainder of the reserves received are excess reserves (column 3). Banks with excess reserves make loans and investments (column 4), creating equal amounts of deposits

	1 Deposits and Reserves Received from Others	2 Reserve Required against Deposits from Others	3 Excess Reserve 1-2	4 Loans and Invest- ments	5 Deposits Created	6 Reserve and Deposits Lost to Others	7 Reserve Remain- ing	8 Deposit Remain- ing
Bank A	1,000,000	150,000	850,000	850,000	850,000	850,000	150,000	1,000,000
Stage 2	850,000	127,000	722,500	722,500	722,500	722,500	127,000	850,000
Stage 3	722,500	108,000	614,000	614,000	614,000	614,000	108,000	722,500

(column 5). The connection between excess reserves, making loans, and creating deposits is indicated by the arrows from column 3 to column 4, and from column 4 to column 5. The deposits thus created are lost to others when borrowers write checks. The arrows from column 6 to column 1 indicate that the deposits and reserves lost by one group of banks are gained by another. Column 7 and column 8 indicate that each bank is left with reserves which are just 15 per cent of its deposits, as required.

The cumulative results of these stages are shown in the following table:

Banks	1 Deposits Created	2 Total So Far	3 Loans and Invest- ments Made	4 Total So Far	5 Total Reserves	6 Required Reserves against Deposits Created	7 Total So Far
Federal Reserve	$1,000	$1,000	—	—	$1,000	$150	$ 150
Stage 1	850	1,850	850	850	1,000	128	278
Stage 2	722	2,572	722	1,572	1,000	108	386
Stage 3	614	3,186	614	2,186	1,000	92	478
Stage 4	522	3,708	522	2,708	1,000	78	556
Stage 5	444	4,152	444	3,152	1,000	67	623
Stage 6	377	4,529	377	3,529	1,000	57	680
Stage 7	320	4,849	320	3,849	1,000	48	728
Stage 8	272	5,121	272	4,121	1,000	41	769
Stage 9	231	5,352	231	4,352	1,000	34	803
Stage 10	197	5,549	197	4,549	1,000	30	833
Stage 20	46	6,448	46	5,448	1,000	7	961
Final	—	6,667	—	5,667	1,000	—	1,000

The first column shows the deposits created at each step of the process, including the initial security purchase by the Federal Reserve System. Except for the first entry, the column is the same as column 5 in the preceding chart. The second column shows the sum of the deposits created up to and including the completion of each stage. The next two columns show the loans and investments made at each stage of the process and their sum. The final two columns show the reserves required against the deposits required at each stage and the sum to date.

You can see that the total deposits created grows larger and larger as the process continues, but the *additional* amount created is growing smaller and smaller. At the same time, more and more of the initial $1,000 of new reserves is being absorbed into required reserves. Also notice that the ratio of total required reserves (column 6) to total deposits created (column 2) is always just 15 per cent.

Eventually all the $1,000 of additional reserves will be absorbed into required reserves, and $1,000 will equal 15 per cent of the total deposits created. So $\dfrac{\$1,000}{.15}$ = total deposits created. Or total deposits created $= \dfrac{\$1,000}{.15} = \$6,667.$

If you examine this same chart, you can see how total deposits approach that limit. At the end of the first 10 steps, $5,549 worth of deposits have been created. At the end of the first 20 steps, $6,448 worth of new money has been created.

The process is shown graphically in Fig. 1. More generally, we can tell the amount of deposits created by any given amount of reserves at any required reserve ratio by the formula

$$\text{Total deposits created} = \frac{\text{New reserves}}{\text{Reserve ratio}}$$

FIG. 1 Cumulative expansion in deposits on basis of $1,000 of new reserves and reserve requirements of 15 per cent.

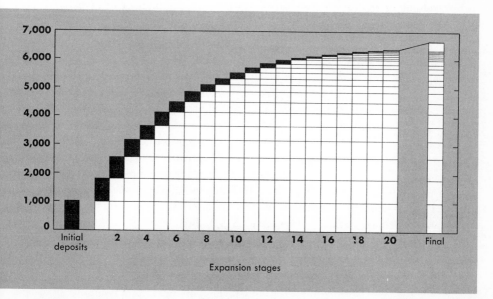

The Federal Reserve System by buying securities can set in motion at any time the multiple expansion process we have just described. Since it can also sell securities, it can reverse the whole process if it wishes.

Suppose the Federal Reserve Bank of New York sells $1 million worth of securities to a large corporation. The buyer pays with a check on bank *A*. The Federal Reserve Bank charges (reduces) bank *A*'s reserve account by $1 million, and bank *A* reduces the customer's account when it receives the check. Bank deposits and reserves have both been reduced by $1 million. But bank *A*'s required reserve has declined by only $150,000. If it had no excess reserves before, it now has a reserve deficit of $850,000. Bank *A* will try to make up the deficit by selling securities. If bank *A* sells securities to customers of another bank, it will gain reserves which the other bank loses. The second bank will now have to deal with its loss of reserves. See if you can follow through the remaining steps of the process of deposit contraction.

VARYING RESERVE REQUIREMENTS

The Board of Governors has another powerful instrument for controlling the money supply and the volume of bank loans and investments. The Board can change the required ratios of reserves to deposits. The power to vary reserve requirements was first granted in 1933. Currently, the Board is empowered to set reserve requirements with the following limits:

On demand deposits	
Reserve and central reserve city banks	10 to 22 per cent
Country banks	7 to 14 per cent
On time deposits for all banks	3 to 6 per cent

The amount of demand deposits which can be supported by a given volume of reserves is $\dfrac{1}{\text{Required reserve rate}} \times$ amount of reserves.

The amount of demand deposits which can be supported by a given volume of reserves is twice as large when the reserve ratio is 10 per cent as when it is 20 per cent. Thus even small changes in required reserve percentages can have a substantial effect on the volume of bank deposits.

A change in the required reserve ratio from 20 per cent to 19 per cent would increase potential total demand deposits by 1/20, or 5 per cent.

The reaction to the change in reserve requirements follows a series of steps, as does the response to an open-market operation. When reserve requirements are lowered, a portion of existing bank holdings of required reserves becomes excess reserves. For example, suppose bank reserves were $20 billion, demand deposits $100 billion, and the required reserve ratio 20 per cent. A reduction of the required reserve ratio to 19 per cent would reduce required reserves to $19 billion, leaving banks with $1 billion of excess reserves. Banks can make loans or buy investments to the tune of $1 billion, creating $1 billion of new demand deposits in the process. The creation of $1 billion of new deposits will absorb $190 million of the excess reserves into required reserves, but leave $810 million of excess reserves. After that, the process will continue in the same way as in an open-market operation.

Three Instruments for Controlling the Money Supply

The volume of bank deposits which can be created by the banking system depends on (1) the volume of bank reserves, and (2) the average required ratio. The Federal Reserve System controls the second factor directly. By means of open-market operations, the system can control the volume of unborrowed reserves. The system exercises control over borrowed reserves by controlling the discount ratio charged member banks and by warning banks which borrow too much for too long.

By *variable reserve requirements, open-market operations,* and the *discount rate* the Federal Reserve System can place an upper limit on the volume of demand deposits. Controlling the upper limit of bank deposits is nearly the same thing as controlling the actual volume of deposits, since it is ordinarily profitable for banks to buy securities or make loans when they have excess reserves.

Monetary Policy and Economic Activity

By controlling the money supply, the Federal Reserve System can exert a strong influence on the course of economic activity. In recessions everyone wants to encourage investment expenditures to check the decline in aggregate income and expenditures. The Federal Reserve System contributes to that objective by using its powers over the money supply. Federal Reserve action and its effect can be summarized as follows:

1. The Federal Reserve System can: (a) reduce discount rates, (b) buy securities in the open market, and (c) reduce reserve requirements.

2. Banks use their increased resources to buy bonds and at the same time become more willing to lend to businesses or to lend on mortgages to home-builders.

3. When banks start to buy bonds, interest rates on bonds tend to fall.

4. Credit is therefore cheaper and more readily available, which encourages businesses to invest and makes it easier and cheaper to buy or build houses. Investment expenditures tend to rise.

5. The "multiplier" effects of increased investment expenditures lead to further increases in income and expenditures.

During booms, when inflation threatens, the Federal Reserve System may act in the opposite direction—to check the growth of expenditures by raising discount rates, selling in the open market, and raising reserve requirements. The whole sequence then works in the opposite direction.

That is a drastically oversimplified account of how Federal Reserve policy affects the economy. In the next chapter we will look more closely at the response of banks to changes in Federal Reserve policy. Then we can consider in Chapter 5 how the response of banks is communicated to the rest of the economy through its effects on financial institutions and other lenders and borrowers.

Summary

In the preceding two chapters we traced the evolution of our monetary system from commodity money to pure debt money. At the same time, we documented the long struggle for control of the money supply. Metallic money, money supplied by unregulated private banks, and the national banking system all proved defective in one way or another.

The present system may be summarized as follows: (1) The bulk of our currency consists of Federal Reserve Notes, which are essentially the same as the private bank notes described earlier. However, the Federal Reserve Banks have a monopoly of note issue and Federal Reserve Notes are not for practical purposes convertible into anything else. Banks always have to be prepared to pay out notes to depositors who ask for them, but banks can always get additional notes from Federal Reserve Banks. When a Federal Reserve Bank supplies notes to a member bank, it charges that bank's reserve account. (2) Over two thirds of our money supply consists of demand balances at commercial banks. The total volume of demand deposits depends on the volume of reserves and the legal reserve ratios. The Federal Reserve System controls legal reserve ratios directly. It can control the volume of reserves by open-market operations and by changing the discount rate. By the use of these three instruments, the system therefore controls the volume of demand deposits.

This system is free of the mechanical defects which plagued earlier monetary systems. The money supply does not depend on the chance discovery of gold, nor is it rigidly limited by an arbitrary rule, or subject to wild gyrations of a free banking regime.

4

THE MODERN COMMERCIAL BANK

So far we have been concerned with the process by which banks create money. Now it's time to take a closer look at the practical operation of modern commercial banks. This is not such an easy task because commercial banking is a large and complex industry. It has come a long way from the days of the wildcat banks.

There are over 13,000 banks in the United States, varying in size from banks like the Chase Manhattan Bank and the Bank of America, with over

$10 billion of assets, to banks with less than $1 million of assets. The nature and scope of their activities also vary widely. Some large city banks are primarily banks for business and have relatively few individual accounts. Others have tried to develop their retail business with individuals by establishing many branches. They have tried to make their services readily available by extending banking hours and establishing branches in subway stations and supermarkets and in many other ways.

All commercial banks accept deposits, make loans, and invest in securities, but banks engage in many other activities. They act as trustees and executors for wills and as investment counsel, underwrite securities, collect bills, rent safe-deposit boxes, and buy and sell foreign exchange. Commercial banking is a major industry in terms of employment and value of services produced. Over 700,000 people were employed by commercial banks in 1963, and the estimated value of the services of banks was over $7 billion.

Although they perform social functions of great importance, banks, like other private businesses, are operated for profit. The basic source of bank earnings is the fact that a bank can earn a higher rate of interest on its assets—loans and investments—than it must pay to its depositors. The excess of interest received over interest paid can be used to pay the costs of operating the bank, and what remains is profit to the bank's stockholders.[1]

Banks do not pay interest on demand deposits, but to induce businesses and households to hold deposits without receiving interest, banks give their services free or at less than full cost. Bank service charges do not cover the full cost of check transfers, record-keeping, rendering statements, and so on. The difference is covered by the net earnings on loans and investments.

Although banks do not pay interest on checking accounts, they usually do offer to pay interest on time (or savings) deposits. Demand deposits can be transferred from one person to another by check, but time deposits cannot. The owner of a savings deposit must present his pass book at the bank to withdraw his funds. He can take away currency or get a bank check which he can deposit in his checking account.

Because it's relatively inconvenient to withdraw funds from savings accounts, most people use them only when they expect to keep their funds on deposit for some time. The amount of savings deposits held by a bank doesn't fluctuate much, so a bank can invest in mortgages or other long-term assets which usually earn more interest than short-term loans.

Commercial banks are in competition for savings deposits with mutual savings banks and savings-and-loan associations. In the last few years there has been intense competition among these institutions, and interest rates on

---

[1] The interest received by a bank is not, of course, all available to cover the costs of servicing deposit accounts. Though they are generally conservative investors, banks take some losses on their loans and investments. Moreover, to avoid losses, a bank must pay the cost of credit investigation, security analysis, and so on. In the case of mortgage and consumer loans, there are substantial costs involved in receiving monthly payments, returning statements, and checking on delinquent borrowers.

savings accounts have increased while depositors have been wooed with advertising campaigns and offers of free clocks and ball-point pens.⌐

Problems of Bank Management

To cover its costs and make a profit, a bank must lend its funds at interest. In seeking to earn a profit it naturally wishes to invest in assets yielding the highest net return. But in making its investment choices it must be constantly aware of its obligation to its depositors. It must be prepared at all times to meet its legal reserve requirement by maintaining the required deposit balance at the Federal Reserve Bank. It must maintain enough vault cash to meet the day-to-day changes in the flow of currency into and out of the bank. In addition, it must have in cash, or in assets which can be readily sold at a predictable value, enough funds to meet deposit withdrawals. Finally, it must conduct its whole investment policy in such a way as to keep losses from bad debts or unsuccessful investments at a very low level.

Every investment involves some risk of loss. And investments offering high returns are generally more risky and less easily turned into cash than those offering low returns. Bank managements must continually balance the need for safety and liquidity against their desire for higher earnings. A bank which never takes any risk of loss on an investment cannot earn enough to cover its operating costs. But a bank which gambles on high-return investments may fail.

Bank Failures

Bank failures have been rare in the last few years. The problems of maintaining enough liquid assets to meet deposit withdrawals and of avoiding excessive losses on loans and investments may not look very serious these days. But we have only to look at the record of the 1920's and the early 1930's to see that they are very real problems. During the prosperous 1920's, banks failed at a rate of over 500 a year. Most of the failing banks were very small, and they held only about 3 per cent of total deposits. With the onset of the depression, the failure rate rose sharply; 1,300 banks failed in 1930, 2,200 in 1931, and 1,400 in 1932. By the beginning of 1933, several state governors closed all the banks in their states, and in March, 1933, President Roosevelt declared a national "bank holiday." All the banks were closed for a time. Most of them were then permitted to reopen and the public was assured that those licensed to reopen were solvent.

The banks which failed during the 1920's and in the early period of the depression had, for the most part, been badly managed. They had failed to maintain enough assets which could be readily sold to meet withdrawals of deposits. Some had taken heavy losses because they had placed all their eggs in one basket—e.g., loans to local farmers. When farm income in the area declined, the bank was bound to fail. Some large city banks had invested heavily in doubtful securities during the boom of the 'twenties.

The failure of large numbers of badly managed banks finally undermined public confidence in the whole banking system. Once the public became really frightened and began to withdraw deposits *en masse,* the strong fell with the weak. Perfectly solvent banks and banks with cash and readily saleable assets sufficient to meet any normal contingency could not meet the panic demand for cash.

Bank Regulation and Deposit Insurance

The disastrous experiences of the early 1930's produced a number of important changes in the banking system.

First of all, the disaster itself swept away a large number of very small, badly managed banks. The number of banks in the United States had risen from about 9,000 in 1900 to over 30,000 in 1920. It had already fallen to 24,000 by 1929 and by 1933 was reduced to about 15,000. Most of the banks which appeared and disappeared were very small, and they held only a few per cent of total deposits; but their failures helped to destroy confidence in the banking system. The reduction in the number of very small banks did a good deal to strengthen the banking system.

Secondly, regulatory standards were generally tightened. Banks have always been regulated, of couse, but they have been regulated more closely since 1933.

Every bank must obtain a charter either from the federal government or from the state in which it operates. To obtain a charter, the incorporators must provide a certain minimum amount of capital, demonstrate that the officers and directors are competent to operate a bank, and have records of financial honesty. In addition, they must show that there is some need for additional banking services in the area in which they propose to operate.

Regulation does not stop there, however. The national banking act and state legislation impose certain limitations on the investments which banks can make. For example: a national bank cannot buy common stock (except of other banks), or lend an amount equal to more than 10 per cent of its capital and surplus to a single customer. Similar regulations are laid down in state statutes. The banking authorities regularly examine the banks in their jurisdiction, not only to audit their books but also to check the adherence of each bank's management to "sound banking practice" as conceived by the examining authorities. Bank examiners may reprimand banks which buy low-quality bonds, or acquire too many loans which go into default, or have to be continuously renewed. They require banks to have sufficient capital and surplus to absorb any losses which the bank may take on its loans or investments and so protect the depositors from loss. Any bank which continuously flouts the recommendations of examiners may have its charter suspended, although, in practice, few ever do.

The reduction in the number of banks and the tightening of regulations governing the creation of new banks and the operation of old ones have greatly reduced the incidence of bank failures. But the experience of the 'thirties showed that even sound, well-managed banks can fail if their depositors become sufficiently frightened. To solve that problem, a system of deposit insurance was developed. In 1934 the Federal Deposit Insurance Corporation was established. Over 97 per cent of all commercial banks, holding 99 per cent of commercial bank deposits, are insured by the F.D.I.C. Each bank pays an annual premium of ¼ per cent of deposits, and in return the F.D.I.C. insures all deposit accounts up to $10,000 per account. In the event of a bank failure, the F.D.I.C. takes over the bank's assets and pays off the depositors. Runs on insured banks have become a rarity—a tribute to the public's confidence in deposit insurance.

Managing Bank Funds

Deposit insurance and bank regulation protect depositors from loss as a result of panic or poor management or both. But the management of the individual bank is still responsible for maintaining the bank's solvency, for maintaining the bank's ability to meet deposit withdrawals, and for earning enough from loans and investments to cover the bank's operating costs and earn a profit for the stockholders. The amounts of some of the most important bank assets and liabilities are shown in Table 4.

TABLE 4

All Member Banks, December 28, 1962 (Millions of dollars)

Assets		Liabilities	
Vault Cash	$ 3,263	Demand deposits	$139,393
Reserves with Federal		Time deposits	80,075
Reserve Banks	17,680	Capital and surplus	19,854
Loans	118,637		
U.S. securities	52,968		
Total assets	$249,488	Total liabilities	$249,488

Maintaining Liquidity

The first task of a bank management is to meet the legal reserve requirements and to be prepared to meet deposit withdrawals. Banks must be prepared to meet their customers' requests for currency without question and must therefore keep coin and currency in their vaults.

Of course, some customers are depositing currency while others are withdrawing it, so that most currency withdrawals can be met from currency deposited on the same day. But deposits and withdrawals never balance exactly. When currency withdrawals exceed deposits, a bank makes payments from its reserve of vault cash. When necessary, it can obtain more cash from its district Federal Reserve Bank or branch—which will charge its account for the amount of currency supplied. When currency deposits exceed withdrawals, a bank will let the cash in its vault build up until it seems worthwhile to send the excess to the Federal Reserve Bank.

Deposit losses through withdrawals of currency are always relatively small, but banks must also be prepared to deal with withdrawals by check. In a unit banking system in which even the largest bank has only a small percentage of total deposits, individual banks find their deposits fluctuating continuously. Small rural banks are subject to sharp seasonal fluctuations, whereas larger banks are subject to erratic changes in deposits as a result of the operations of their large corporate customers. For example, a large corporation may accumulate several million dollars in a New York bank then pay it all away in dividend checks, most of which will be deposited elsewhere. Or a corporation will raise several million dollars by selling securities and deposit the proceeds in its principal account. In these operations, one bank's deposit gain is another's loss, but each bank must make its own adjustment to the change.

When a bank suffers a net loss of deposits, its account at the Federal Reserve will be charged that amount. If it formerly held exactly the required reserve, it will now have less than the required reserve. For its deposit at the Federal Reserve will be down $1 for every $1 withdrawn, whereas its required reserve is down only $.15, if the required reserve ratio is 15 per cent. It therefore has a deficit in its reserve account of $.85 per dollar of deposit loss. To be prepared to meet deposit losses, therefore, a bank must either carry deposits at the Federal Reserve in excess of the legal requirement or be prepared to replenish its account at the Federal Reserve Bank very quickly. Many small banks do carry excess reserves as a normal procedure. But, since deposits at the Federal Reserve earn no interest, that is a relatively costly way of preparing for deposit withdrawals.

In addition to their vault cash and deposit with the Federal Reserve Bank, most banks maintain deposits at other banks. Banks in small towns and cities maintain balances with banks in larger cities. They may draw on those balances to meet deposit withdrawals. In addition, they receive many kinds of services, such as investment advice, safe keeping of securities, and processing of checks, from their city correspondents.

Vault cash, excess reserves, and deposits with other banks are one line of defense against deposit losses. In addition, most banks try to prepare for deposit withdrawals, without losing too much interest, by investing in securities which can be readily sold with no risk of loss. For this purpose the ideal instrument is a federal security due to mature in a short time.

There is no risk of default on these securities, and if they are due to mature shortly their prices cannot fluctuate much. There is an active, well-organized market in these securities, and the cost of buying and selling them is very low. By holding securities of this type, a bank can earn interest and still be prepared to meet deposit losses. If deposit losses do occur, it sells part of its short-dated federal securities to other banks or their customers. It will receive payment by check on another bank, and, when it sends that check to its Federal Reserve Bank it will have its account credited, thus offsetting the loss of deposit at the Federal Reserve Bank which occurred earlier.

A bank suffering from deposit losses may also borrow from its Federal Reserve Bank. Assuming that the bank is not already in debt, it can obtain a loan from its Federal Reserve Bank without much question, pledging government securities against the loan. The Federal Reserve Bank will credit the commercial bank with the amount of the loan and thus increase the reserve of the commercial bank by enough to eliminate its reserve deficit.

CHOICE AMONG ALTERNATIVE RESERVE ADJUSTMENTS

Individual banks are constantly gaining or losing deposits and must take frequent action to adjust their reserve positions. A bank which loses reserves must choose whether to draw on its excess reserves (if any), draw on balances with correspondent banks, sell securities, or borrow from its Federal Reserve Bank. Banks which gain reserves may choose to repay debt to the Federal Reserve, to buy securities, or build up correspondent balances or excess reserves.

In choosing whether to borrow or sell securities, a bank must consider the cost of borrowing. If the discount rate is above the going interest rate on short-term government securities, the bank will find it cheaper to sell securities than to borrow. If the discount rate is below the rate on short-term securities, it will pay to borrow. However, banks must limit their Federal Reserve borrowing. Even if a bank finds it profitable to borrow from the Federal Reserve for an extended period, it cannot always do so. A bank which borrows too much for too long will find itself subject to pressure from Federal Reserve officials to get out of debt.

A bank which gains reserves will usually repay at once if it is in debt to the Federal Reserve. If it is not in debt, it may wish to rebuild hitherto depleted balances with correspondent banks. Otherwise, unless it anticipates a loss of reserves, it will ordinarily buy securities when it gains reserves.

In adjusting their reserve positions to meet the legal requirement while keeping their funds fully invested in interest-earning assets, banks buy and sell millions of dollars' worth of securities every day. And individual banks are constantly borrowing from or repaying their Federal Reserve Banks. Most of these transactions cancel out. One bank loses deposits, another gains. One bank borrows from the Federal Reserve, another repays. All that activity is simply part of the process of transferring ownership of demand deposits in all sorts of business transactions.

But there is also a cyclical pattern to the reserve adjustments of the banking system as a whole. In recession, the banking system as a whole repays debt to the Federal Reserve System and builds up excess reserves. At the same time, the banking system as a whole is buying securities. During the upswing of the business cycle, banks generally increase their debt to the Federal Reserve System, reduce excess reserves, and sell securities. This pattern is the result of the response of the banking system to the actions of the Federal Reserve and to the changing loan requirements of its customers. It can be understood more fully after we have examined the other assets held by banks.

Loans and Investments

Once a bank has met its legal reserve requirements, provided an adequate supply of vault cash, placed sufficient deposits with correspondents, and acquired enough highly liquid securities to meet possible deposit losses, it may use the balance of its funds to make loans or to buy other securities.

In placing its funds, a bank must not only conform to the legal restrictions mentioned above but also must confine itself to loans and securities of the highest quality. A bank cannot afford to gamble. Subject to that qualification, banks naturally prefer to invest their funds in assets promising the highest yields.

The nominal interest rate, however, is not always the ruling consideration. Interest charged on consumer installment loans is much higher than on other loans or securities, but the interest earned is partly offset by the costs involved in those loans. State and local securities are a better investment for a bank than corporate securities, even though nominal interest rates are lower, because the interest on state and local securities is tax free. Finally, and perhaps most important, the net gain from making loans to deposit customers is only partially measured by the interest received on the loan.

LOANS AND CUSTOMER RELATIONSHIPS

The relationship between a bank and its business deposit customers is a continuing one, not a series of isolated transactions. A business firm keeps deposits with a bank for years at a time, and the bank is able to earn interest as a result. The bank in turn performs services such as processing wage and dividend checks without charge. It may also supply financial advice, credit information, and other incidental services. If the customer's average deposit balance is more than sufficient to cover the average cost of the services provided by the bank, the customer is valuable to the bank. When such a customer asks for a loan, the bank is very much inclined to accommodate him if it can possibly do so. The bank feels that if it refuses loans to good (i.e., profitable) deposit customers, the customer is likely to take the first opportunity to establish a new banking connection. Of course, a customer who keeps an average balance of $10,000 cannot expect to borrow a million dollars. There has to be some relationship between the size and profitability of a customer's balance and the size of the loan he can expect to get. But subject to that condition, and when the customer's financial prospects justify the loan, banks give first priority to the loan requests of good deposit customers in allocating their funds. When loan demand is increasing more rapidly than deposits, a bank will be prepared to sell off securities, even at a loss, to accommodate its good-customer loan requests.

However, banks whose loan demand fluctuates over the business cycle try to avoid having to sell securities at a loss to accommodate loan demand. When business is poor and demand for loans is low, they invest part of their resources in relatively short-term securities, even though they could get a higher yield on longer-term assets. During an upsurge in the business cycle, the short-term securities bought during the slump will mature or can be sold with little loss and the proceeds used to increase loans to customers.

CONSUMER LOANS

Loans to individuals—personal loans or installment credit connected with the purchase of durable goods—do not ordinarily involve an important customer relationship of the type described above. People who take installment credit do not ordinarily have large bank accounts. However, these loans generally give banks a better return than almost any other kind of asset.

Because of its profitability, most banks are anxious to develop their consumer-loan business. They have done so by engaging in advertising campaigns and acquiring branch offices. And, as bank-lending to consumers has grown, banks have built up special staffs and personnel to handle the business. Once a bank has built up a market position, it is reluctant to risk losing it by turning away business. When the demand for consumer loans expands, banks generally try to accommodate it—selling off securities if necessary. Thus, the fluctuations in demand for consumer loans pose problems for bank managements which are similar to those caused by fluctuations in loans to business customers.

Other Assets

The assets just mentioned are particularly important for an understanding of the cyclical changes in the distribution of bank assets. But, banks have many other kinds of assets. They make many loans to business firms and to individuals whose deposits do not warrant a priority status.

In addition to their holdings of relatively short-term United States securities, banks hold large amounts of other bonds. They hold around $10 billion worth of U.S. securities having over 5 years to run and a smaller amount of corporate securities. Because they are tax exempt, the securities of state and local governments have been very attractive to banks in recent years, and commercial banks hold about $20 billion worth of these bonds. Finally, banks in suburban areas and city banks with large branch systems hold large amounts of mortgage loans.

The amount a bank can invest in long-term bonds and mortgages depends mainly on three factors.

1. *The stability of its deposits.* If a bank's deposits do not fluctuate much, it needs a relatively small reserve of short-term securities to meet deposit withdrawals. Since time deposits do not usually fluctuate as much as demand deposits, a bank with a large proportion of time deposits may, if it wishes, hold a relatively large proportion of long-term bonds and mortgages.

2. *The proportion of its assets absorbed by the loan requirements of the deposit customers.*

3. *The extent to which the bank has built up its consumer-loan business.*

When business and consumer-loan demands are expanding rapidly, banks acquire relatively few of these longer-term assets. During periods of business contraction, when bank reserves are expanding rapidly, banks have used part of their increased resources to buy municipal securities, long-term United States securities, and mortgages.

Cyclical Movements in Bank Assets

We have noted a number of ways in which banks respond to changes in loan demand and changes in Federal Reserve policy. We can now review those adjustments and tie together the reactions of individual banks with the behavior of the banking system as a whole.

During recession periods the Federal Reserve usually reduces required reserve ratios or buys securities to increase bank reserves. In those periods most banks are gaining reserves. Any banks which owe the Federal Reserve can repay it. Once out of debt, a bank with increased reserves or lower required reserves can buy securities or make loans. Since loan demand is usually declining in recessions, banks with excess reserves buy United States or state and local securities. As far as an individual bank is concerned, it is simply a matter of paying for securities with a check on its Federal Reserve account. But since the check will be deposited in some other bank, the reserve balances do not disappear when they are used. A fraction of them is tied up in additional required reserves with each round of the multiple expansion process. The process works out just as in the examples given in the preceding chapter except that (1) some of the reserves provided by the Federal Reserve are used to repay debt to the Federal Reserve, and (2) some small banks are slow about investing funds so that excess reserves increase in recessions. Deposits and bank assets do not grow as much as our theoretical examples in the preceding chapter would suggest.

During business-cycle upswings, banks find themselves in a quite different position. The Federal Reserve doesn't usually add to the reserves of the banking system during a boom. But demand for business and consumer loans usually expands rapidly. The loan departments of banks respond to the demand by making many new loans—creating additional deposits in the process. The new deposits will be spent quickly so that the banks making loans will lose deposits almost as fast as they create them. And for every dollar's worth of checks drawn on these new deposits, the lending bank will lose a dollar's worth of reserves to some other bank.

The banks which lose reserves in that way draw down excess reserves, use their deposits with correspondent banks, sell securities, or borrow from Federal Reserve Banks. Most of the problem will be met by selling securities to individuals or corporations. When a bank sells a security to a non-bank individual or corporation, the bank is paid with a check on the buyer's account. The volume of bank deposits is reduced and so is the volume of required reserves. When banks makes loans, they create deposits, and when they sell securities, they destroy deposits.

But banks also meet reserve deficits by borrowing from their Federal Reserve Banks. When they do so, the total reserves of the banking system are expanded. An increase in reserves obtained from borrowing provides the basis for a multiple expansion of deposits just as much as an increase in reserves resulting from an open-market operation. Thus the money supply may expand in the upswing even though the Federal Reserve has taken no action at all—except to lend reserves.

The amount of deposit expansion based on borrowing is limited, because the Federal Reserve banks discourage banks from borrowing large amounts or remaining in debt for long periods. An increased demand for bank loans which accompanies a rise in business activity can be partly accommodated by an expansion in bank assets supported by the use of excess reserves existing at the start of the boom and by borrowed reserves. Banks can make additional loans by selling securities to the non-bank public. But those resources are limited. Banks have relatively small amounts of excess reserves even at the end of a recession, and their ability to borrow reserves from the Federal Reserve Banks is limited. The volume of government securities held by banks is very large. But since interest rates are usually rising and security prices falling, only short-term securities can be sold without loss.

As a boom progresses, many banks find that they have sold out most of their shorter-term government securities. They can make additional loans only by taking capital losses on sales of long-term securities. Banks are willing to take some capital losses but not an unlimited amount. They become reluctant to increase their loans. Most banks feel that they must accommodate their good deposit customers, but they refuse loans to others or lend less than the requested amount or for a shorter period.

Variations in Federal reserve policy and in business activity have their effect on the availability of credit through the efforts of thousands of individual banks to adjust their reserve positions and portfolios to changing conditions. When the Federal Reserve supplies banks with additional reserves, banks become eager to expand loans. When reserves are not expanding and loan demand increases, loans become hard to get. Thus part of the varying tension between Federal Reserve policy and business conditions is reflected within the banking system. But since banks sell off securities to make loans, they pass part of the effect of changing conditions onto the rest of the financial markets. We will consider those other markets in the next chapter.

Summary

Commercial banks engage in a great variety of activities, but their main business consists of accepting deposits and investing in loans and securities.

In making their investment decisions bank managements naturally wish to invest in the assets which produce the highest net return (after allowance for investment costs and losses). At the same time, however, they must avoid taking any serious chance of loss which might render the bank insolvent. They must also be prepared to meet deposit withdrawals at any time. They must, therefore, hold a substantial amount of assets which can be readily liquidated. In addition, they must meet legal reserve requirements and hold enough vault cash to accommodate their customers' requests for currency.

When a bank has provided for deposit withdrawals and met legal reserve requirements, it can invest the remainder of its assets in business loans, mortgage loans, installment loans to consumers, or in federal, state and local, or corporate, bonds.

Banks generally give priority to loans to business firms who maintain deposits with the bank. Consumer installment loans have proved particularly profitable to many banks. The demand for business and consumer loans varies over the business cycle. When demand for loans expands more rapidly than deposits, banks sell government securities. In the reverse situation—usually during recessions—banks rebuild their holdings of government securities. Banks also borrow from Federal Reserve Banks during periods when demand for loans is expanding rapidly and repay during recession periods. As a result, the money supply may expand during a prosperous period even when the Federal Reserve Banks are not making any open-market purchases. During recessions part of the reserves provided by the Federal Reserve System are absorbed when member banks repay their debts to Federal Reserve Banks.

During periods when loan demand is expanding rapidly, some banks cannot sell enough securities or borrow enough to satisfy all their customers' requests for loans.

5

CAPITAL MARKETS

The banking system is responsive to changes in Federal Reserve policy and to the changing needs of its customers. The resulting changes in the availability of bank credit have a direct influence on expenditures for goods and services. But the banking system passes on some of the pressures to which it is subjected, by buying and selling securities. Changes in Federal Reserve policy, as well as changes in the demand for loans, are felt in the capital markets outside the banking system.

The capital markets consist of a set of formal and informal markets for securities together with a variety of financial institutions and specialized financial firms—e.g., securities brokers and dealers. The capital markets transfer funds from households, businesses, and governments that have surpluses (save more than they invest) to those with deficits (i.e., that invest more than they save). They also make it possible for wealth-holders to change the form in which they hold their assets, in accordance with their changing needs. The magnitude of the task is indicated by the fact that financial transactions can amount to $2.5 trillion or more in a single year.

Since capital is scarce, the limited amount available must be allocated among competing users. Although there is some rationing in our capital markets, capital funds are allocated mainly by interest rates. Those who are willing to pay the most for borrowed funds outbid the low bidders.

Households, businesses, and governments are all borrowers in the capital markets and they are all lenders as well. The amounts they want to borrow reflect changes in income, and changes in government expenditures, incentives for business investment, and, in the case of households, demand for housing and consumer durables. Over the course of the business cycle, the amount of funds raised by the different sectors changes rapidly. You can get some idea of the magnitude and volatility of the different types of demand for capital funds by examining Fig. 2.

The capital markets must continually adjust to these changing pressures

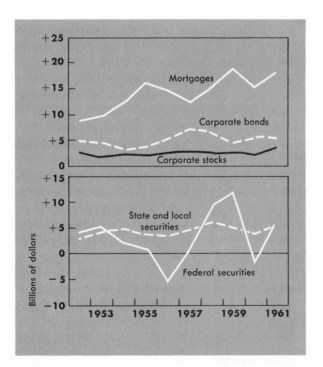

FIG. 2 Net new issues of market instruments. (Source: *Federal Reserve Bulletin,* May, 1962.)

in order to maintain a balance between the demand and supply for each type of security and in the market as a whole. That adaptation is achieved through changes in interest rates and the responses of lenders and borrowers to them.

Interest rates influence in three ways the amounts borrowed and lent:

1. They influence the rate of business expenditure for plant and equipment and the rate of residential construction. When businesses invest less, they usually borrow less (or lend more). When families buy fewer houses, they borrow less on mortgages.

2. Differences in interest rates on different kinds of securities influence the way in which borrowers obtain their funds and the places where lenders invest their funds. Thus, changes in interest rates draw money from markets where funds are plentiful to markets where they are scarce.

3. People who save can lend their money or retain it. And borrowers can increase their holdings of money by borrowing more than enough to finance expenditures. Interest rates influence the amount of money people want to hold and thereby the amount they lend or borrow.

Interest Rate and Investment Expenditures

We shall first consider the reactions of investors to changes in interest rates. The two largest categories of investment are business investment in plant and equipment and residential construction.

BUSINESS INVESTMENT

In a growing healthy economy there is bound to be a large volume of business investment in plant and equipment. In recent years business plant and equipment investment has amounted to about $50 billion per year.

Investment decisions. The management of business firms are constantly faced with decisions involving investments. They must decide whether to expand capacity or use overtime work to increase output. They must decide whether to replace old machinery with new equipment, whether to bring out a new product line or modify an old one. In all these decisions they must weigh the gains from reductions in labor or materials cost, or additions to revenue, against the cost of the capital goods which produce the cost savings or added revenues. In doing so, they are faced with the fact that they must spend money *now* to save money *in the future.*

In deciding whether to buy new capital equipment or buildings, managements must first consider whether the cost of the capital goods will be covered by the reduction in labor, material, or other costs resulting from its introduction (or by the value of additional output produced). Since capital goods last a long time, it's necessary to add up the cost savings for each of a number of years and compare the total with the cost of the equipment. Obviously it is never worthwhile to invest unless the total savings (or additional revenue) produced are enough to cover the cost of the equipment.

But is that enough? If a machine cost $1,000 and saved labor costs of $100 per year for 10 years, would anyone buy it? Of course not. No one wants to trade $1,000 now for $100 each year for 10 years. We all prefer money now to money in the future. If the machine is going to be worth buying, it must produce more than just enough to cover its cost over its lifetime.

By how much must the revenues produced by a piece of capital exceed the cost? Any one person or firm will have to decide by considering what else he could do with his money. To any one individual or firm, money in the future is worth less than money now because he can lend out money at interest now and get more back in the future. The value now of $1 a year hence is not $1. It is the amount you need to invest now at the going interest rate to get $1 a year from now. Suppose the going interest rate is 5 per cent. Every dollar invested now will bring $1.05 in 1 year. To get $1 a year from now, you need to invest $1/1.05 = $.952. The amount $.952 is called the *present value* of $1 in 1 year discounted at 5 per cent.

How about $1 two years from now? Every dollar invested now will bring $1.05 at the end of the first year. In the second year you earn interest on the first year's interest, so that at the end of the second year you will have $1.05 × $1.05 = $1.1025. To get $1 at the end of 2 years you need to invest now $1/1.1025 = $.907. You can get the present value of $1 discounted at 5 per cent for any number of years by dividing $1 by $(1.05)^n$, where n is the number of years. Figure 3 shows how present value declines as

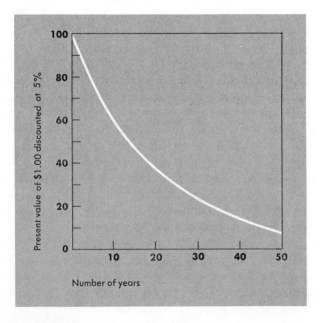

FIG. 3 Decline in present value with increase in number of years of discounting.

the number of years of discounting increases. Of course, you can work out the same calculation for any rate of interest. For instance, the present value of $1 discounted for 1 year at 8 per cent is only $.926, and for 2 years it is only $.857. You can see that the present value of money to be received in the future declines as the interest rate rises. And the decline in the present value caused by a rise in the interest rate increases with the length of time involved.

A business firm making an investment has to compare the capital expenditure involved with the sum of the present values of the returns from the investment in future years. The decision rule is: Make the investment *if* sum of present values of future returns is *greater* than capital outlay required to get them. An increase in interest rates reduces the present value of the prospective returns for each future year. Some investments which would pass the test at a 4 per cent rate of interest will fail to pass it at a 5 per cent rate.

Every year business firms are faced with thousands of decisions regarding investment. The necessity for making those decisions is an inevitable part of business life in a growing and changing economy in which demand grows and shifts from one kind of product to another, while new equipment and new production methods are constantly being developed. In all problems involving investment, the level of interest rates will influence the final decision. For in all those choices an investment now will save dollars in the future (or a larger investment will save more future dollars than a smaller one). In making decisions, it is necessary to compare the present value of the dollars to be saved in the future with the investment to be made now. And as we have just seen, projects which would be profitable at a low interest rate will not be profitable at a higher one.

Consider the investment decisions that have to be made in a particular year. If in that year the interest rate is around 5 per cent, the various choices might result in business decisions to spend $35 billion for the year on plant and equipment. If the interest rate were 6 per cent instead of 5 per cent, most of the cost calculations on most of the individual choices would come out the same way. But in a certain number of cases, the difference between a 5 per cent interest rate and a 6 per cent rate may take a project out of the barely worthwhile category, and put it in the unprofitable category. So if the interest rate were 6 per cent (all other circumstances the same), the rate of expenditure for plant and equipment might be, say, $33 billion for the year. And if the rate of interest were 4 per cent, some projects which were unprofitable at 5 per cent would become worthwhile, so a 4 per cent rate might be associated with, say, $37 billion of plant and equipment expenditure for the year. Figure 4 shows the amount of investment which might be made in a given year, at each of a number of different interest rates.

The examples just given and Fig. 4 are hypothetical. Investment varies from year to year for many reasons. It changes with the rate of capacity utilization, with changes in technology, with businessmen's outlook for the future, and a variety of other factors.

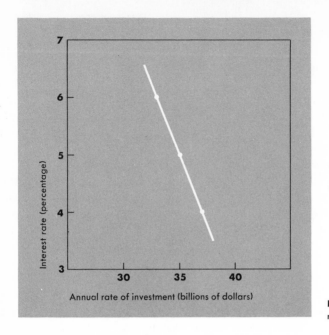

FIG. 4 Effect of interest rates on investment.

Nonetheless, one might suppose that a sufficiently low rate of interest would open up an almost unlimited volume of investment opportunities. After all, there should be an enormous number of projects which would save enough labor to cover their cost given a long enough time. If the interest rate were zero or next to zero, would not all those long-term projects become profitable?

Actually, most of them would not. The fact that money can be lent out at interest is only one reason for regarding a future dollar as worth less than a present one. The future dollars to be earned by buying buildings and equipment are only potential, hypothetical dollars. They may or may not actually be received. A dollar now is a *certain* dollar. A dollar in the future is necessarily an uncertain one. No investment project is guaranteed to yield a return or even recover its cost. The demand for the product of particular buildings and equipment may disappear. The technique embodied in specific equipment may become obsolete any day from tomorrow onward.

Most firms, then, view the future returns from investment with considerable skepticism. Many of them take the attitude that an investment is not worth making unless it promises to yield enough revenue to cover its costs in, say, 5 years. And no one is willing to make an investment whose expected return is no greater than obtainable from buying a bond.

Moreover, the source of funds used to finance investments makes a difference. As a matter of arithmetic, it does not make any difference whether one pays interest on borrowed money to finance an investment in plant or equipment or forgoes receiving interest by financing it with one's own funds. But a firm runs the risk of getting into financial trouble if it borrows to finance investment projects. The prospective return from an investment project must not only cover interest costs but must be high enough to compensate the firm financing with borrowed money for the extra risk involved.

Moreover, firms may not be able to borrow all they want, particularly in tight-money periods. Since rising interest rates and credit rationing go together, it's sometimes difficult to distinguish between the effect of interest rates on the demand for credit and the effect of rationing on the availability of credit.

The interest rate is only one of many factors influencing the rate of investment. Variations in interest rate account for only a small part of the total variations in the rate of investment. To determine the net effect of changes in interest rates on investment, we have to use elaborate statistical studies. A number of such studies have been made, but there is still considerable disagreement concerning the change in investment induced by changes in interest rates. The upshot of the studies made, however, suggests that a change in the level of interest rates of 1 per cent (e.g., from 4 per cent to 5 per cent) will change the annual rate of business investment by $1 billion or $2 billion. Some economists think the effect may be substantially greater; others, that it may be much smaller.

FINANCING HOMES

Home-ownership has become a basic element in the pattern of American life. About 60 per cent of American families own their own homes, a proportion which has risen rapidly in the post-war years. Many factors have contributed to this trend, but it would not have been possible without the new arrangements for home-financing developed during the depression and immediately after World War II.

Home-ownership inevitably requires borrowing. Relatively few families, particularly in the age groups in which people wish to acquire their first homes, have enough assets to pay for a house. They have to borrow, and the usual way of borrowing is to mortgage the house being purchased. Most of the home-financing loans are provided by savings-and-loan associations, mutual savings banks, life insurance companies, and commercial banks (especially those with large amounts of savings deposits). Individuals do extend a substantial amount of mortgage credit, but the proportion of mortgages taken by individuals is much smaller than before the Great Depression. A mortgage borrower may deal directly with a local lender but if he buys a house from a large-scale builder, the builder may arrange the mortgage financing.

Lenders usually require borrowers to make a "down-payment" on the house. That is, the lender will lend only a fraction of the purchase price. Until a few years ago, lenders typically required down payments of 30 per cent to 40 per cent of the purchase price, but in the last few years, many lenders have been willing to accept down payments of as little as 20 per cent.

Most mortgages today are "amortized." A payment schedule is arranged so that a constant monthly payment covers interest and repayment of the principal over a period ranging from 10 to 30 years. At the outset, most of the monthly payment is required for interest, and only a fraction of the payment is used to reduce the principal of the loan. As the amount outstanding declines, the interest charge becomes smaller and the amount paid on the principal increases. As time passes, the borrower's equity (value of the house less debt) tends to increase. Of course, the required monthly payment increases with the interest rate and decreases as the payment period increases (Table 5).

TABLE 5

Monthly Payments on a $20,000 Mortgage

Interest Rate (Percentage)	20 Years	15 Years
4	$121.20	$147.94
4½	126.53	153.00
5	132.00	158.16
5½	137.58	163.42
6	143.29	168.78
6½	149.12	174.23

You can see from the table that the monthly payment required to buy a house costing a given amount increases as the interest rate increases. Mortgage payments are a substantial part of the total expense of owning a house.

When interest rates rise, potential home-buyers have to make a choice between taking less housing or reducing their expenditures on other things. Some of them will decide not to buy a new home or to buy a less expensive one. Thus an increase in interest rates tends to reduce the rate of residential construction.

GOVERNMENT INSURANCE AND GUARANTEE

Many people who want to buy a house and can afford large enough monthly payments to carry a mortgage for the full value of the house do not have funds to make a substantial down payment. They are, therefore, unable to obtain ordinary or "conventional" mortgage financing.

In an effort to stimulate home-building, the federal government established the Federal Housing Administration in the 1930's and authorized FHA to establish a program of mortgage insurance. For a premium of ½ per cent of the principal, FHA insures mortgage lenders against loss. Lenders are willing to lend on FHA insured mortgages with little or no down payment. The Veterans Administration operates a mortgage guarantee program for veterans which is similar to the FHA program.

In an effort to protect borrowers from exploitation, Congress imposed maximum, or "ceiling," interest rates on FHA and VA mortgages. This regulation has some peculiar effects on the availability of mortgage credit. When market rates rise, however, lenders find it unprofitable to lend at the "ceiling" rates imposed by Congress and place their funds elsewhere. People who do not have money for a substantial down payment are then unable to secure financing and are unable to buy houses.

In the post-war period, changes in interest rates have caused substantial fluctuations in the rate of residential construction. Those fluctuations reflect (1) the influence of interest rates on cost of home ownership, and (2) the influence of interest rates on the availability of credit to potential buyers.

Thus both the major categories of investment expenditure—business investment and residential construction—are adversely affected by a rise in interest rates and stimulated by a decline in interest rates.

Reactions of Lenders

As we have just said, the amount of funds that each kind of borrower wants or can get is influenced by interest-rate movements. Lenders also respond to changes in interest rates and can be induced to lend more in one place and less in another by changes in the returns in different kinds of assets. In an efficient capital market, all borrowers are competing for a common pool of funds. That will occur if lenders are willing to shift from one kind of security to another in response to small changes in the interest rates and different kinds of securities. We must now look at the responses of lenders to changes in interest rates.

Households are the largest suppliers of-funds in the capital markets, but businesses and governments and banks also are important contributors. State and local governments supply funds to the capital markets because they operate pension funds for their employees. The federal government has a number of lending agencies which extend credit to farmers, small businesses, and others. Businesses supply funds because large firms lend to small ones, because they offer consumer credit, and because they hold reserve funds in the form of government securities.

Since households are the most important contributors to the flow of funds into the capital markets, we shall give primary attention to their financial investment decisions.

FINANCIAL INVESTMENTS OF HOUSEHOLDS

Every individual saver wants to invest his funds in a way which is consistent with his own needs and plans. Some people are primarily concerned with keeping what they have and are willing to take a low return on their investments if they can get security of principal. Others are willing to take some risk of loss in return for higher dividend or interest income. Still others are interested in capital gains over long periods and are not much concerned with current income. People in high tax brackets want to get their investment returns in forms which minimize their tax payments. Some people have funds to invest for short periods and want to be able to get their money quickly and easily when they need it. Others are investing for the long pull and do not worry about quick liquidation of their investments.

On the other side of the coin, capital funds are needed by many different kinds of borrowers—by businesses large and small, governments, home-builders, and people wanting credit for durable-goods purchases. Each of them wants to raise funds in ways which suit his needs. The saver looking for an outlet for his funds finds that literally thousands of stocks and bonds and mortgages offering different degrees of safety, interest, or dividend returns are available. Some types of investment (e.g., residential mortgages) require a lot of work in collecting payments, inspecting the property, and seeing that taxes are paid. Others can only be made successfully by someone willing to go to the trouble of investigating the borrower's credit rating. Still others require extensive technical knowledge.

THE PATTERN OF FINANCIAL ASSETS OF HOUSEHOLDS

Corporate stock makes up about half of the value of financial assets held by households. And the value of common-stock holdings is now over four times as great as at the end of World War II. That enormous increase reflects the change in value of existing stocks in response to increases in corporate earnings and confidence in the future. The net value of corporate stock purchased by households has been relatively small (see Fig. 5).

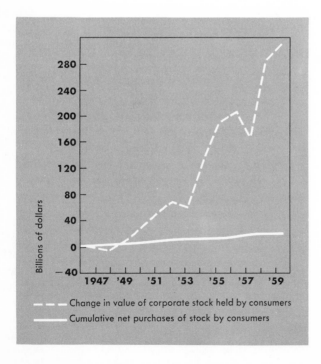

FIG. 5 Net value of corporate stock purchased by households, 1947-1959. (Source: *Business Review,* Federal Reserve Bank of Philadelphia, October, 1960.)

Households buy bonds of corporations, of state and local governments, and of the federal government, along with some mortgages. But aside from United States Savings Bonds, their direct holdings of bonds and mortgages make up a small fraction of their financial assets. The remainder of their assets takes the form of claims against financial institutions—demand and savings deposits at commercial banks, deposits in mutual savings banks, savings-and-loan shares, and claims against pension funds and insurance companies. And a very large part of the current savings of households goes into these institutions. Some major changes in the financial assets of consumers are shown in Fig. 6. Recent movements in the flow of consumer savings are shown in Fig. 7.

The Growth of Financial Institutions

The rapid growth of financial institutions reflects some basic changes in the development of the American economy. With the growth of the economy and with the progress of industrialization and urbanization, the investment choices facing the public have become more complex. At the same time, the number of families who can save, but who do not own a farm or business, has increased. A number of types of financial institutions have

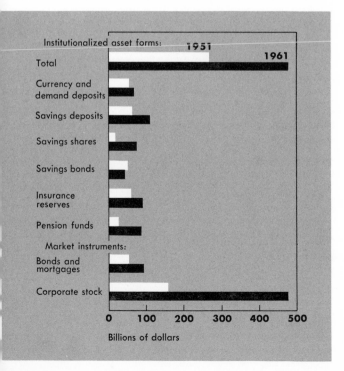

FIG. 6 Financial assets of consumer sector. (Source: Federal Reserve Bulletin, May, 1962.)

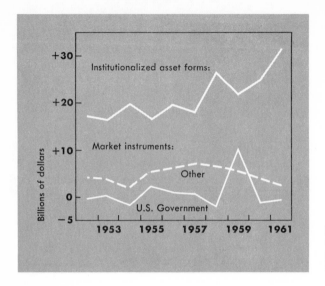

FIG. 7 Consumer acquisitions of financial assets. (Source: *Federal Reserve Bulletin*, May, 1962.)

developed to serve the needs of these investors. They include life insurance companies, pension funds, mutual savings banks, savings-and-loan associations, and mutual investment funds, as well as commercial banks. Although many of those institutions have existed for a long time, their growth has been very rapid in recent years. A large proportion of individual savings now flows through these institutions.

Each of these institutions exists to provide some specialized service to investors, but they all help to reduce the risks and cost of investment for individual savers through (1) advantages of scale, and (2) diversification.

Advantages of scale. A careful investor must investigate the securities he buys and make comparisons among alternative investment opportunities. This takes time and trouble and may cost money. The job of security selection costs the same whether the amount to be invested is a million dollars or a thousand dollars. Moreover, a financial institution investing large sums can afford to hire specialized personnel to investigate and select securities.

In the field of mortgage-lending, financial institutions have an advantage over individual lenders. Experience with large numbers of loans enables savings-and-loan associations and savings banks to appraise properties and evaluate borrowers' ability to pay much more effectively than any individual lender. This consideration has become increasingly important as the size of cities has grown. A wealthy individual in a small town may know local property and the credit standing of his neighbors as well as anyone. But only a professional can judge the quality of mortgages in Los Angeles.

Second, the thrift institutions service mortgages throughout their lives. They collect monthly payments, make sure that taxes and insurance are paid, and periodically inspect the properties to see that they are maintained. If the borrower has difficulty making payments, the institution has the staff to make arrangements for refinancing or to take legal action to avoid losses. All these functions can be performed more cheaply on a wholesale basis by a professional staff than by individual lenders. In short, a large financial institution can do a better job of investment management and selection at a lower cost per dollar invested than can an individual.

Diversification. Because of the costs of security selection, most individuals must limit their investment to a relatively small number of securities. A large financial institution invests in a very large number of securities. The wisest investors make mistakes. But when one out of the hundreds of bonds held by an insurance company goes into default, the loss as a percentage of total assets is very small. Each security held by an individual investor, on the other hand, is a significant part of his total holdings. A loss on a single security can be critical to an individual holding only a few securities, but negligible to a large institution with hundreds of different securities.

All types of financial institutions provide the public with the advantages of large-scale operation and diversification. In addition, each type of financial institution has its own function and has grown for some special reason. Thus life insurance and pension funds provide a family with financial security—by providing retirement income and protection against the loss of the family's principal earner. The need for protection of that kind has increased with industrialization, urbanization, and increasing length of life.

THRIFT INSTITUTIONS OFFER LIQUIDITY

Holders of deposit funds and shares of mutual savings banks and savings-and-loan associations expect to be able to convert their deposits into money at any time. The thrift institutions are able to fulfill that expectation in spite of the fact that most of their assets are invested in mortgages which run for a long period and cannot be readily sold. Thrift institutions hold small amounts of liquid assets—demand deposits and short-term government securities—in case withdrawals should exceed deposits. But thrift institutions have been growing for many years and withdrawals seldom outrun deposits. Thus the holder of a thrift deposit has an asset which he can convert into cash on very short notice.

Thrift institutions have grown rapidly because of their ability to provide investors with professional management, diversified assets, and liquidity. The need for their services has increased with industrialization and urbanization.

Given those basic sources of growth, the savings institutions have been able further to improve their ability to attract savings by advertising, opening new offices, and increasing the range of services offered. Financial institutions now play a major role in the process of transferring funds from households with funds to lend to households, businesses, and governments who want to borrow. And because they are professionally managed and alert to small differences in investment returns, they play a major role in the process of allocating loanable funds among competing borrowers.

Competition for Funds

All the major borrowers in the capital market—businesses, the federal government, state and local governments, house-builders, and other consumers—compete with one another for the available funds. That competition is most obvious in the case of publicly issued bonds. Existing securities of the federal, state, and local governments and of corporations are actively traded. Any issuer of a new security must offer an interest rate which makes a sufficient number of buyers want that security rather than any of the others they could buy.

But borrowers compete with one another even when there is no active market for their securities. There is no regular market for mortgages. But insurance companies and savings banks will not lend on mortgages unless they can charge an interest rate which compares favorably with the return they could get if they bought bonds instead. Commercial banks with long-term funds to invest compare the returns on mortgages against those on state and local bonds.

There are other less direct forms of competition. Thus savings banks and savings-and-loan associations invest heavily in mortgages. But mortgages compete with marketable bonds for the funds of savers.

A rise in bond yields induces people to buy bonds instead of making deposits at thrift institutions. Indirectly, this draws funds away from the mortgage market. Mortgage rates must be high enough to enable the thrift institutions to compete effectively for savings.

There is also competition among different kinds of securities through choices made by borrowers. Large business firms may borrow by selling bonds or by borrowing from banks. Finance companies have the same choice. The competition among different types of securities is sufficiently intense to make most interest rates move together. There are differences in the levels of rates because securities differ in terms of risk, because some have special tax advantages, and for many other reasons. But the interest rates on different kinds of securities do move together. Some move more readily than others. And there are persistent geographical differences in mortgage rates and bank lending rates.

Our capital markets are by no means perfect, but capital funds generally do go to those who are willing to pay the most for them. That is the essential requirement for an efficient allocation of capital resources among competing users. Competition among borrowers and lenders insures (subject to some qualifications) that any given total of available capital funds will

FIG. 8 Fluctuations in demand and supply and interest rates. The graph above shows the interest rates that are most responsive to fluctuations, while the graph below shows those that are less responsive. (Source: *Federal Reserve Bulletin,* September, 1962.)

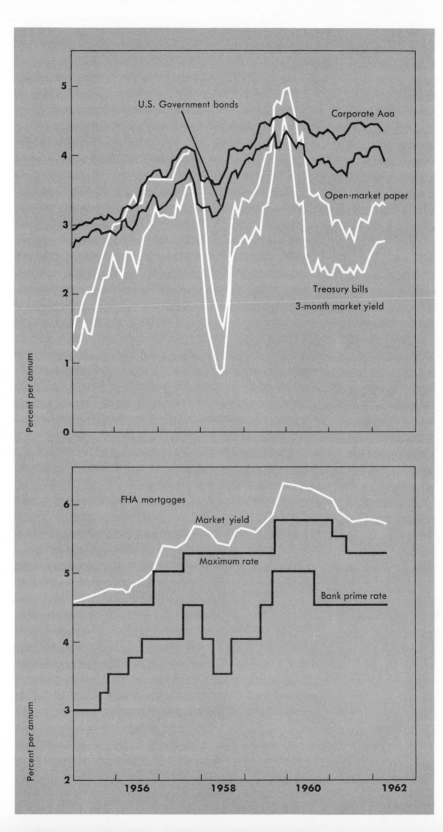

be distributed among potential borrowers in a reasonably efficient way. Those who are willing to pay the most for funds will get them, others will have to do without.

Summary

Our capital markets and financial institutions serve a great variety of households, businesses, and governments who seek to lend or to borrow.

Financial institutions, such as mutual savings banks and savings-and-loan associations, investment trusts, insurance companies, and pension funds, reduce the costs and risks of investment. Their size makes it possible for them to hold diversified portfolios and to select and care for their assets at a low cost per dollar invested. Mutual savings banks and savings-and-loan associations also provide their customers with liquidity. Urbanization and industrialization and the increasing human life span have increased the need for life insurance and pension funds.

Financial institutions as well as many individual investors are sensitive to changes in the interest yields from different kinds of securities. When an increased demand for funds pushes up interest rates on any one type of security, some investors will sell another kind of security to buy the one whose yield has risen. As a result, all interest rates move up and down together, although some move more quickly than others. And we may regard all kinds of borrowers as in competition with one another for a common pool of funds. When borrowers generally seek to obtain more funds, all interest rates tend to rise.

The movements of interest rates are important because investment decisions are influenced by interest rates. Business firms find investment projects more attractive when interest rates are low than when they are high. And the cost of owning a house is reduced when interest rates fall. Everyone agrees that changes in interest rates influence the rate of residential construction and the rate of business investment in fixed plant and equipment. But there is a good deal of controversy over the size of the effect of a change in interest rates on investment expenditures.

6

SUPPLY AND DEMAND FOR MONEY
AND THE LEVEL OF INTEREST RATES

We have described how funds are drawn from one sector of the capital market to another by relatively slight changes in the differences between interest rates. Let us now turn our attention to the determination of the level of interest rates and to the effect of the level of interest rates on investment and national income.

Differences in interest rates reflect the competition between one kind of security and another kind. From the standpoint of the investor, securities not only compete with one another, but also with money.

Any investor or potential investor always has the option of holding money or any other kind of asset. Savers may use their funds to buy securities or to invest in claims against financial institutions. But they may also simply build up their holdings of demand deposits. People who are not currently saving always have the option of selling the financial assets they hold and adding to their holdings of money.

Business firms finance investment by borrowing. But they can, if they wish, sell securities in excess of the amount required to finance investment and use the excess to add to their holdings of money. And, of course, if households and businesses want to reduce their money holdings, they will act in the opposite way.

The level of interest rates must be precisely high enough to induce households and businesses to hold all money in existence. If interest rates are too low, households and businesses will add to the supply of securities or reduce the demand for securities in an attempt to add to their money holdings. This will drive up interest rates. People who most want additional money will get it, while those who least want money will give it up in return for higher interest earnings. Collectively they will not increase the total holdings of money. Only the banking system can do that. If bank reserves are increased, banks will bid for bonds and drive down interest rates until someone is willing to part with bonds in exchange for money.

In effect, then, the interest rate must be at a level which equates the supply and demand for money. We have already studied the supply of money. Let us now consider what determines the demand for money.

Household Demand for Money

There are three general motives for holding money: (1) the transactions motive, (2) the precautionary motive, and (3) the speculative, or portfolio balance, motive.

TRANSACTION MOTIVE

Everyone wants to have some funds in a conveniently available form, because the time pattern of income receipts does not match the time pattern of expenditures. People may receive most of their income in monthly payments and spend a considerable part of it within the month. They will obviously hold most of the unspent balance in demand deposits or currency.

Some income may be received quarterly or annually and some expenditures (e.g., insurance and tax payments and vacation expenditures) may be on an annual cycle. Funds *from* large infrequent receipts and *for* large infrequent payments may be held either in demand deposits or in some form of savings deposits or shares. Thus the household demand for money and "near money" tends to rise with the level of personal income and consumer expenditure.

Money may also be "tied up" in the process of trading assets. People are constantly buying and selling common stocks and other assets. When one man sells a stock to another, the seller receives money which he is likely to hold for some time before he decides how to reinvest. He may hold a demand deposit until he makes his decision or he may acquire a savings deposit to earn some interest in the interim. Thus the demand for money and "near money" is likely to rise with the amount of wealth which can be transferred from one person to another.

PRECAUTIONARY, OR CONTINGENCY, MOTIVE

Life is full of unpredictable problems. Cars break down, houses need major repairs, people become ill. And the solution to most of those problems involves money. Many people have to borrow to meet unexpected expenditures. But most people who have substantial assets like to have funds readily available to buy a car or repair the roof. They could hold all their assets in stocks and bonds and either sell them or borrow against them when the need arises. But most people are willing to give up some interest and hold a demand deposit or a savings deposit to enjoy the feeling of security that comes from having funds available without having to worry about the state of the market.

PORTFOLIO BALANCE, OR SPECULATIVE, MOTIVE

Many people are never able to accumulate financial assets which provide more than enough for day-to-day transactions and a modest contingency reserve. And the great bulk of American families never succeed in acquiring more than a few thousand dollars of financial assets. They are likely to hold their assets in money or near-money form. Most of those families find that the time and trouble and risk involved in buying stocks and bonds outweigh any gains in income they might obtain.

People with large amounts of assets generally invest in many other assets besides money and savings deposits. But they also hold substantial amounts of savings deposits. The rich need contingency reserves like anyone else. In addition, they may be "balancing" more risky investments by holding part of their assets in a very safe form.

At any one moment there are some wealthy individuals who want to hold most of their wealth in the form of cash or something close to it. They may believe that securities prices are going to fall or they may feel so uncertain about the future of securities prices that they take a "wait and see" position by holding cash. The force of the "speculative motive" for holding money or near money varies greatly over time. Ordinarily, the amount of money held for speculative reasons is small. But in times of panic large numbers of people may try to get out of securities and into cash.

Demand for Money and Liquid Assets Relative to Income

As income rises, the amounts households want to hold for all purposes tend to increase. Transaction requirements tend to rise in rough proportion to the volume of transactions. The amount that is needed to cover the risk of illness, unemployment, and other contingencies increases with the standard of living. And, of course, the aggregate amounts needed for those purposes increase with the growth of population.

The amount of liquid assets required for asset management is not directly connected with income but to wealth. But it is certainly true that wealth grows with income. Thus there is a general tendency for the demand for liquid assets to grow in proportion to income. But many other factors also influence the need for liquid assets. Transaction requirements may change with changes in payment methods. People who are paid weekly will hold less money on the average than those who are paid monthly. The use of credit cards, charge accounts, and installment credit may reduce cash holdings. Unemployment insurance and health insurance and the availability of installment credit reduce the need to save for emergencies. On the other hand, people are able to set aside more for such contingencies as their incomes rise.

Finally, the amount of liquid assets people want to hold varies with confidence about the future. People who worry about unemployment or business losses certainly will hold more cash than people who expect steadily rising incomes.

Competition between Money and Other Liquid Assets

Most of the reasons for holding liquid assets can be served by holding currency, demand deposits, savings deposits, savings-and-loan shares, or United States Savings Bonds. All these assets provide a person with a means of holding wealth in a form which guarantees the dollar value of the asset and which is readily available.

But demand deposits are more convenient than any of the others. You can write a check against a demand deposit. You cannot spend any of the other assets without first converting them into money—e.g., by pre-senting your passbook at a savings bank, getting a check from the savings bank, depositing the check with your commercial bank, and *then* writing a check.

On the other hand, you do not receive interest on demand deposits as you do on the other forms of liquid assets. It costs something to have the greater convenience of demand deposits. The "price" of holding demand deposits is the amount of interest lost by not using one of the other forms of liquid assets.

Obviously, the significance of the convenience of demand deposits and the income from other forms of liquid assets varies with the purpose for which the assets are being held. If your only liquid asset is the unspent portion of the check you received on the first of the month, there is not much point in keeping it in a savings account. You would have to go to a lot of trouble to make withdrawals every time you want to pay a bill or get some currency. In any event, you would not receive much interest, if any. On the other hand, a man who has saved $5,000 for a "rainy day" is in a different position. He can earn $50 a year even if the savings deposit rate is only 1 per cent. And he earns it with very little trouble because he hopes, at any rate, that "rainy days" won't come very often. In between, of course, there are people who hold varying sums in liquid form for varying lengths of time. We generally expect that people who hold large sums in liquid form for long periods of time will hold them in a form which yields interest. Small sums held for short periods will be held in demand deposits and currency.

But as the interest rate on savings deposits and other non-money liquid assets rises, we expect the proportion of liquid assets held in money form to decline. At a 1 per cent interest rate, a person earns $50 on a $5,000 deposit. At 4 per cent $1,250 will earn $50 a year, as will $5,000 held for 3 months. As interest rates rise, then, we expect savings deposits to attract funds held for short periods or in smaller amounts and therefore to attract a greater share of the total.

(During the late 1930's the interest rates offered by thrift institutions were very low and the shares of currency and demand deposits in the total liquid assets of households reached 35 per cent. Since the end of World War II, the share of currency and demand deposits in total liquid assets of households has fallen almost continuously. It is now below 20 per cent. Only a part of the change can be attributed to interest rates, but there seems to be little doubt that the post-war rise in interest rates has induced households to hold less money in relation to their income and wealth.)

Business Demand for Money and Liquid Assets

Businesses hold large amounts of money and liquid assets and for the same general reasons as do households. Businesses need funds for ordinary, day-by-day transactions because their receipts and expenditures are differently timed. During certain parts of the month or certain seasons of the year, they receive more than they pay out, and at other times they pay out more than they receive. Business firms take care of variations in receipts and expenditures by borrowing at some times of the year and re-paying at others. But unless the treasurer wants to borrow or repay every few days, he needs a substantial cash balance for operating purposes.

Businesses also hold liquid funds for precautionary purposes. Every business wants to be able to survive a slack period without going bankrupt. And every business wants to be able to take advantage of favorable investment opportunities without borrowing.

Finally, businesses have a speculative motive for holding liquid assets. When interest rates appear abnormally low, corporate treasurers may borrow and build up liquid assets. They expect to use those funds later when interest rates are higher.

Businesses also have a choice between holding money and other liquid assets. They may hold money or they may hold Treasury bills or time deposits. And like households, they will switch from cash into other liquid assets when interest rates rise enough to make it worth the cost and inconvenience.

Supply and Demand for Money and the Level of Interest Rates

[At any given level of income and wealth, households and businesses will want to hold a certain amount of liquid assets. As interest rates rise, a progressively greater share of household liquid assets will be held in the form of savings deposits, savings bonds, or savings-and-loan shares. And as interest rates rise, businesses will tend to hold a higher proportion of their liquid assets in the form of treasury bills or time deposits and a smaller proportion in the form of cash.]

THE DEMAND CURVE FOR MONEY

Households and businesses want to hold more money when interest rates are low, rather than when rates are high. The demand curve for money looks like any other demand curve, with the interest rate as the price of money (see Fig. 9).

We have already mentioned that, at a given interest rate, the need for money increases as income and wealth increase. People need more money for ordinary day-to-day transactions, and contingencies, and more money is allocated to buying and selling assets as income and wealth increase. The curve in Fig. 9 is drawn for a given level of income and wealth. At higher levels of income and wealth, more money would be required at each level of interest rate. Not one schedule, but a whole series, one for each level of income and wealth, relates interest rate and demand for money. In Fig. 10

FIGS. 9, 10   Demand for money related to interest rates and income.

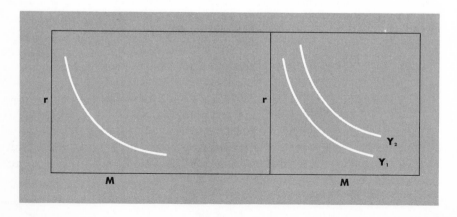

the curve marked Y_1 represents demand for money at one level of income; Y_2 is the demand for money at a higher income.

DETERMINING THE INTEREST RATE

We can regard the supply of money as being determined by the Federal Reserve System. Since it is independent of the interest rate, we represent it as a vertical line in Fig. 11.

At any given level of income and with any given supply of money, the interest rate is set at the intersection of the supply and demand for money. In Fig. 11 the money supply is M_1. At the interest rate r_1, people are just willing to hold that amount of money.

EFFECT OF A CHANGE IN MONEY SUPPLY

If the Federal Reserve should increase the supply of money, the supply curve would shift to the right and supply and demand for money would be equated at a lower level of interest rates. Thus in Fig. 11 an increase in the money supply from M_1 to M_2 reduces the interest rate from r_1 to r_2.

THE EFFECT OF A CHANGE IN INCOME

Suppose, on the other hand, that the level of income were to rise while the supply of money remained constant. Then the whole demand schedule for money would shift upward to the right. Supply and demand for money would be equated at a higher level of interest rates.

In Fig. 12 the money supply is M_1. The demand for money is shown by the curve marked Y_1. The equilibrium interest rate is determined by the intersection of the vertical line M_1 with the curve marked Y_1 at point a. The interest rate is r_1. An increase in income increases the demand for money at every level of income. The new demand-for-money curve is Y_2. It intersects M_1 at point b, so the new equilibrium interest rate is r_2.

FIGS. 11, 12 Effect of changes in money supply and income on interest rates.

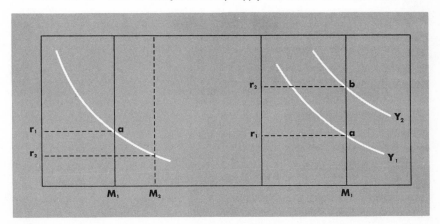

ADJUSTMENTS OF INTEREST RATE TO INCOME CHANGE

If expenditures and income are to rise without an increase in the money supply, then businesses and households must be induced to remain content with a constant volume of money even though the value of transactions has increased. A higher rate of expenditure means more employment at higher wages and consequently more money in people's pockets, and more money held in bank accounts between the receipt of wages and their expenditure. Businesses too will have more in their cash registers and will be piling up larger bank balances in preparation for the payment of wages and other bills. And, if the higher level of income persists for a time, people will wish to hold more liquid funds for contingency purposes. At the same time, the value of assets will rise and the amounts of money tied up in the purchase and sale of assets will tend to increase.

Something has to give. Households that want more cash can get it by not lending all their savings. Businesses that want more can get it by borrowing more than they need to finance investment. *But not all of them increase their holdings of money simultaneously.* Competition for the limited supply of funds—in the form of efforts to borrow or refusals to lend—will drive up interest rates. Those who find it least inconvenient to do so will be willing to earn interest (or avoid paying) by getting along with less money. Thus those who need to increase their cash position most and who are willing to pay for the privilege will get more of the limited supply of money.

The interest rate is the price of holding money, and it responds like any other price. An increase in expenditure increases the demand for money —shifts the demand curve to the right. If the supply of money is fixed, the price (interest) rises.

Interest Rates and Investment

We mentioned several ways in which changes in the level of interest rates influence investment expenditures.

1. Some investment projects which would be profitable at a low rate of interest are not worthwhile undertaking at a higher rate.

2. An increase in interest rates generally occurs when banks are in a tight reserve position. When security prices are falling and banks are indebted to the Federal Reserve, some business borrowers have difficulty in obtaining bank financing.

3. An increase in market interest rates raises the cost of owning a house and therefore reduces demand for housing. An increase in interest rates also draws funds away from thrift institutions and reduces the profitability of mortgage lending. An increase in interest rates therefore has an adverse effect on residential construction.

Money Supply and National Income

The Federal Reserve controls the money supply, the money supply influences interest rates, and interest rates influence investment. By increasing or decreasing the money supply, the Federal Reserve can influence the rate of investment. And the rate of investment is an important determinant of the level of income.

Let us review the process of income determination. Figure 13 summarizes the national income determination process. Line CC is the consumption function, which shows the amount of consumption expenditures which will be made at each level of national income. We can add a constant amount to that line for government expenditures. Thus $C + G$ shows the sum of consumer and government expenditures at each level of national income. The consumption function must be drawn so as to reflect the impact of the tax system on consumer income and expenditure.

Finally, we can add the investment expenditures associated with each level of income to the other two kinds of expenditures. That gives us $C + G + I$ in Fig. 13. The equilibrium level of income is reached at the point a where $C + G + I$ crosses the 45° line so that gross national expenditure equals GNP.

The rate of investment at each level of national income depends in part on the level of income of interest rates. And the level of interest rates at each level of income depends on the money supply. So by *increasing M*oney we get a *lower* level of interest rates at each level of income and a *higher* supply level of *investment* at each level of income.

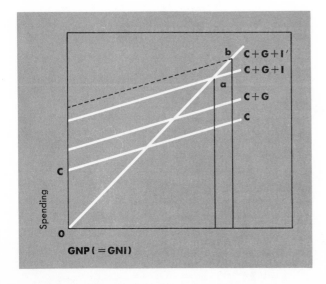

FIG. 13 The national income determination process.

The line $C + G + I$ in Fig. 13 corresponds to one particular money supply. If the money supply were larger, the rate of investment at each level of income would be higher. The effect of an increase in money supply is shown by shifting the expenditure line to $C + G + I'$. In Fig. 13, $C + G + I'$ intersects the 45° line at point b, a higher level of GNP.

Notice that the increase in GNP resulting from the increase in investment is greater than the increase in investment. This reflects the multiplier effect of a change in investment on income.

Monetary Policy and Full Employment

The achievement of a satisfactory level of employment is one of the major goals of economic policy. At one moment a certain value of total output—GNP—corresponds to any given rate of unemployment. To hold unemployment down to a satisfactory level, total expenditures must equal potential GNP at the chosen level of unemployment. In Fig. 14 the level of national income marked *FE* corresponds to a 4 per cent level of unemployment. That level will be achieved if the $C + I + G$ line crosses the 45° line at point a over point *FE*. The line $C' + I' + G'$ yields an equilibrium level of income lower than *FE* and results in too much unemployment. The line $C'' + I'' + G''$ produces an equilibrium level of income to the right of *FE*. There is too much demand and consequently too much inflation.

Notice that what counts is the *total* of consumption plus government expenditures plus private investment expenditures. If the total is too high or too low, policy measures are available which will raise or lower any one of the three components.

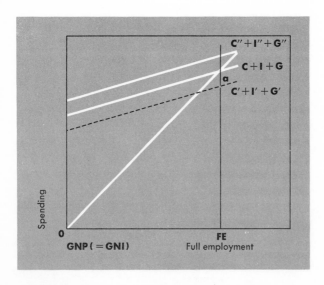

FIG. 14 Total spending required for full employment.

Taxes can be raised or lowered to raise or lower the consumption function, and government expenditures can be raised or lowered. The money supply can be increased to raise I or reduced to lower it. Other measures such as changes in business taxes can also be used to raise or lower I.

Thus, monetary policy is one of a set of instruments which can be used in achieving the full-employment goal. The appropriate use of any one instrument of policy depends on the way in which the other policies are used.

For any given fiscal policy, some particular rate of investment is required to achieve full employment. The line $C + G$ in Fig. 15 shows the consumption plus government expenditure at any level of income resulting from a particular combination of government expenditures and taxes. Given that fiscal policy, the task of monetary policy is to produce an investment demand which makes $C + G + I$ pass through a point a above FE. Tighter money would generate too much unemployment.

The distance ba—the excess of full-employment income over consumption and government expenditure at full employment—is the potential *full-employment saving* of the economy. It represents private saving at a full-employment income plus government saving (which may be positive or negative). The task of monetary policy is to find a level of interest rates which exactly equates investment demand with full-employment saving.

The problem facing the monetary authority is illustrated in Fig. 16 (a) and (b). Line I in (a) shows the level of investment associated with different levels of interest rates out of full-employment increases. The vertical line S shows full-employment saving. The interest rate which will make investment equal saving at a full employment income is r_0. The curve marked Y_f in Fig. 16 (b) is the demand for money at a full-employment income level. A money supply of M_0 is necessary to achieve the interest rate r_0.

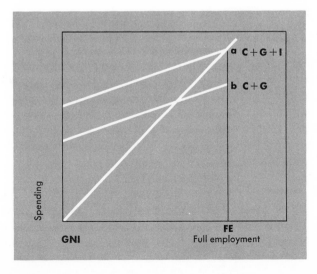

FIG. 15 Rate of investment required for full employment.

The level of full-employment saving depends not only on the level of full-employment income but also on the fiscal policy adopted. Full-employment saving can be increased by reducing government expenditures or by raising taxes. [When the economy is at full employment, government economy or higher taxes can be used to increase full-employment saving. Monetary policy can then be eased to induce more investment and thereby increase the rate of growth of output. Measures to increase full-employment saving *permit* an easier monetary policy.] But notice that they do not cause it. An increase in full-employment saving without an increase in M would lead to a decline in income.

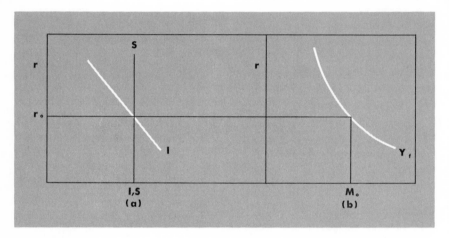

FIG. 16   Money supply required for a full employment rate of investment.

Monetary Policy and Resource Allocation

That comment brings us back to the question of resource allocation. At the end of Chapter 5 we mentioned that the capital markets work so that the funds flowing into the capital market are allocated to those who are willing to pay the most for them. But how much is available in the capital market? Is there a fixed amount of savings to be allocated? We know that there is not. An increase in investment will raise the level of income and of savings. From your study of national income determination, you know that the rate of saving is equal to investment. There is no fixed amount of savings to be allocated among competing investors.

The amount of savings that *should* be allocated among investors is the amount people are willing to save at a full-employment level of income. (If the Federal Reserve provides the right amount of money, a full-employment income will actually be achieved.) The amount of savings generated by that level of income will be efficiently allocated if the rest of the capital markets do their job. But if the Federal Reserve doesn't provide enough money, there will be waste. Some potential investors will be priced out of the market, even though there are idle resources.

The Need for a Growing Money Supply

At any one moment there is a correct level of interest rates and money supply for the existing fiscal policy. But of course the level of money supply required to produce full employment is always changing. As our labor force increases, technology improves, and capital is accumulated, the full-employment GNP increases. The full-employment rate of saving will ordinarily increase along with the full-employment GNP. The rate of investment corresponding to a full-employment level of income and any rate of interest will rise. In Fig. 16 a rise in the full-employment level of income would shift both the *I* curve and the *S* curve to the right. They will intersect at more or less the same level of interest rates. (The movement of the investment curve with the passage of time depends on many other factors besides the change in income. So the rightward shift in the investment curve might be greater or less than the shift in the full-employment savings curve.)

The demand-for-money curve also shifts to the right with a higher level of income. So to keep the interest rate about the same and to absorb the increase in saving associated with increased income, the money supply has to increase through time.

Another Approach: The Quantity Theory of Money

We have been discussing the impact of money on expenditures in terms of supply and demand for money holdings. It is also possible to think about the effects of the money supply on expenditures in terms of the rate of movement of money. People receive money, hold it for a while, then spend it. We may ask either (1) How much money do people want to hold at a given level of income and interest rates? Or (2) How quickly do people spend money after they receive it?

MEASURING THE SPEED OF MONEY MOVEMENT

We can't watch individual dollars move, but we can measure how fast money moves on the average. In 1960 there were $4 trillion worth of money transactions in the U.S. The average amount of money in that year—coins, currency, and checking accounts—was $141 billion. So each dollar changed hands 28 times on the average. The ratio of the volume of transactions to the stock of money is called the *transactions velocity of money*.

Since our primary interest is the relation between money and the output of goods and services, it is also desirable to have a measure of the relation of the stock of money to the annual flow of final purchases of goods and services—the gross national product. The ratio of GNP to the stock of money $\frac{GNP}{M}$ is called the *income velocity of money* (denoted by V). In 1960 the GNP was \$503 billion, so $V = \frac{503}{141} = 3.6$ per year for 1960. The income velocity of money differs from the transactions velocity because it excludes (1) financial transactions, and (2) intermediate transactions. We have counted the payment to the dealer for the finished automobile but left out the dealer's payment to the manufacturer, the manufacturer's payment for steel, and so on.

Income velocity is sometimes called circuit velocity because it measures the times per year that a dollar completes the circuit from income to purchase of goods and services and back again.

THE EQUATION OF EXCHANGE

We have defined the income velocity of money by the equation $V \equiv \frac{GNP}{M}$. We have retained the three-bar equality sign to indicate that the equation is definitional. It's always true because it only restates the definition of V. We can rewrite the equation again by splitting up GNP into its components—prices and outputs. The *value* of the goods and services produced in a year is the product of the physical output of goods and services (O) and their price level (P). So $GNP = P \times O$. The equation $MV = P \times O$ is called the "equation of exchange."

Since the equation is essentially a definition, it doesn't tell us anything about the real world. But it does serve to remind us of some connections between money and other things that must always be true. In particular, any change in M must be accompanied by either a decrease in V or an increase in GNP expenditures and an increase in output, prices, or both.

If V were constant, control of the money supply would mean control of national income and expenditure. An increase in M would imply a proportional rise in either the price level or in the level of output, or in some combination of the two. Moreover, since the potential output of the economy is limited at any time, any very large and rapid increase in M would necessarily produce a more or less proportionate rise in prices. Any substantial contraction in M would spell depression, with declining output and employment and a falling price level. But remember that those conclusions are valid *only if V is constant.* The notion that the level of expenditure and the price level are simply related to the amount of money in existence is called the *quantity theory of money.*

Actually V varies a good deal. Look at Fig. 17. You can see that in 1945 the average dollar went around the income circuit about twice. In

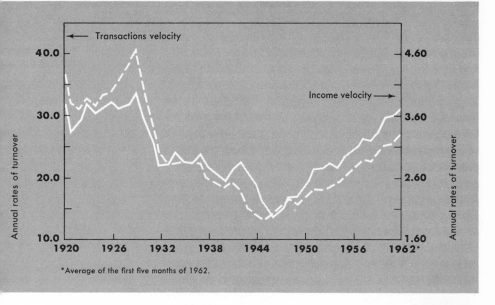

FIG. 17   The velocity of money, 1920-1962. (Source: St. Louis Federal Reserve Bank, *Monthly Review*, September, 1962.)

1929 and 1962 the average dollar went around the income circuit nearly four times a year.⌐

It still may be possible to use the quantity theory approach. We could analyze income flows in terms of the movements of *M and* the movements of *V*. Thus movements in *V* may be caused by changes in the way payments are made. Money moves more quickly if people are paid weekly instead of monthly because people hold less money for ordinary day-to-day transactions. Or velocity may change because of changes in confidence. If people hold money idle because of fear of unemployment, the *average* rate of movement of money will decline.

Thus we could try to explain GNP by explaining the movements of *M* and the movements of *V*. And monetary policy would be directed toward (1) increasing *M* in pace with the growth of GNP, and (2) offsetting movements of *V* by increasing the supply of money when *V* declined, and vice versa.

That approach will not work, however, if changes in *M* or changes in GNP *cause* changes in *V*. In that case the movements of *V* do not cause movements in GNP but reflect them.

Most economists think that is the real situation. Velocity moves in the same general way as the interest rate (see Fig. 18). Most economists explain the movement of velocity in relation to the interest rate in terms of the theory of demand for money outlined above.

If GNP rises, demand for money increases. If the supply of money does not rise or does not rise as fast as income, interest rates rise. A rise in GNP relative to *M is* an increase in *V*. The accompanying rise in interest rates is necessary to induce households and businesses to accommodate their

81

demand for money to the available supply.[1] Similarly, a rise in M causes a decline in interest rates and, simultaneously, a fall in V. If changes in M and GNP cause changes in V, then we can neither treat V as constant nor regard it as an explanation of changes in GNP.

MONEY AND INCOME IN MOVEMENT

So far we have examined the influence of the money supply on the equilibrium level of income under a fixed set of conditions. But the world we observe is one of growth and change. In that world there is a continuous interaction between changes in the money supply and changes in the many other forces working on the level of income and expenditure. It is useful to trace out at least a few steps in that interaction process.

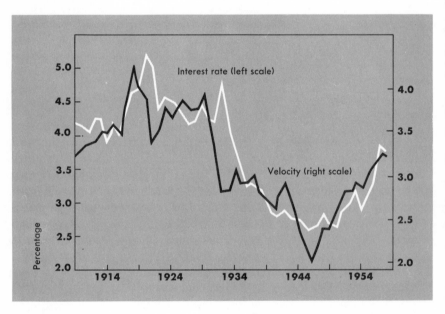

FIG. 18 Annual income velocity compared with corporate bond yields, 1909-1958. (Source: H. A. Latané, "Income Velocity and Interest Rates," *The Review of Economics and Statistics,* November, 1960.)

Suppose that, for some reason, the rate of expenditure on goods and services starts to rise while the money supply remains constant. Government expenditures, for example, might have increased with no change in tax rates. As a result of the increased government purchases, the rate of flow of income to households and businesses will be increased. They in turn will tend to increase their rate of expenditure. Thus there is a tendency for

---

[1] Sometimes the demand for money increases even when income is falling—e.g., during financial panics. Then the interest rate may rise when V falls. This is the explanation for the divergent movements of r and V in 1921 and the early 1930's.

all the elements of GNP (C and I as well as G) to move upward. An initial rise in G will lead directly and indirectly to an increase in GNP. With M constant, an increase in GNP leads to a rise in interest rates.

The sequence may be put in the following schematic way:

$$+ G \rightarrow + I \rightarrow +_C \text{GNP} \rightarrow + r$$

The plus sign indicates a positive change.

So far we have shown that an increase in expenditure occurring when the supply of money is constant leads to an increase in interest rates. But, of course, the money supply does not have to be absolutely constant. If income rises by 10 per cent and the money supply by 5 per cent, interest rates will have to rise. Whenever income is rising faster than money supply, interest rates tend to rise.

We can now expand our causal sequence to take into account the effect of rising interest rates. Our original sequence showing the impact of an increased rate of government expenditure was:

$$+ G \rightarrow + I \rightarrow +_C \text{GNP} \rightarrow + r$$

Now we add a term $+ r \rightarrow - I$ to represent the adverse effect of the rise in interest rates on the rate of investment. The entire sequence now is:

$$\begin{array}{ccccc} (1) & (2) & (3) & (4) & (5) \end{array}$$
$$+ G \rightarrow + I \rightarrow +_C \text{GNP} \rightarrow + r \rightarrow - I$$

The negative change in investment induced by the rise in interest rates offsets the positive acceleration effect of the initial rise in income on investment.

Thus the failure of the money supply to grow acts as a brake on the increase in income induced by the increase in government expenditures. Of course, it does not make any difference whether the sequence is started by an increase in government expenditure or by an increase in private expenditure. The initial force leading to an increase in expenditure might come from a change in technology or the rate of population growth or some other factor favorable to private investment. The sequence would then be:

$$+ I \rightarrow I \rightarrow +_C \text{GNP} \rightarrow + r \rightarrow - I$$

Notice that investment appears in the sequence three times: first, because the initial spending impulse was in the investment area; second, because an increase in income always encourages investment; third, because an increase in interest rates checks investment.

The sequence could even start with consumption if there were, say, a tax reduction for households. It doesn't make any difference where the initial spending impulse comes from. If the money supply does not increase, the last term in the sequence will always be a negative force working on investment.

We have said that a constant money supply operates as a brake, slowing down the growth of expenditure. How effective a brake is it? No general answer is possible. Under some circumstances the monetary brake could be very weak and ineffective. Under others it could be strong enough to prevent income from rising at all without an increase in M. The strength of the brake depends on the relative response of demand for money and investment to the interest rate. Suppose, for example, that (1) it is very easy to induce households and businesses to take substitutes for money, (e.g., savings deposits and treasury bills) in response to a small rise in interest rates; and (2) investment is very insensitive to interest rates. Then a strong impulse toward increasing spending (e.g., an increase in government expenditure or a change in various factors favorable to investment) could drive income up considerably but increase the interest rate only slightly. And the "negative feedback" of the increase in interest rates would have little adverse effect on investment.

But if those interest-rate responses were reversed, a fixed money supply would choke off any tendency for income to rise. Suppose (1) demand for money were very insensitive to interest rates, and (2) investment were very sensitive to interest rates. Then a slight rise in income would cause a large rise in interest rates, which would reduce investment sufficiently to offset the initial impulse to rising income. Of course, the real situation is always somewhere in between. We will discuss some concrete cases illustrating the operation of the monetary brake in the next chapter.

EFFECTS OF CHANGING "M"

We have seen that the money supply is a factor which can influence the economy merely standing still, but, of course, the money supply does change. Suppose M increases at a rate which just keeps pace with the growth of income. In that case M is moving just fast enough not to interfere with the other factors that influence income.

So far we have considered situations in which government expenditure or some force favoring investment is driving income upward. Now let us consider the effect of money when other factors are not driving income upward or downward. Suppose that in those circumstances the money supply is increased, with GNP constant. Then an increasing M implies a fall in interest rates. Interest rates fall as the Federal Reserve and the banks offer money for bonds. They have to drive bond prices up and interest rates down to induce people to hold money instead of bonds. The decline in interest rates will stimulate investment and raise income (which will, of course, increase the need for money, partly offsetting the downward pressure of the rising money supply on interest rates).

How effective is an increase in M in generating an increase in income? Again that is an empirical question and the answer varies. If demand for money is sensitive to the interest rate and investment is unresponsive, an increase in M will not have much effect; but if demand for money does not respond actively to a reduction in interest rates and investment does respond, an increase in M will be useful in starting an increase in income. Exactly the same reasoning applies when we try to bring about a recovery from a recession by increasing the money supply.

With that background we can now proceed to examine the results of Federal Reserve policy actions as they have worked out in practice.

Summary

Interest rates are determined by the interaction of supply and demand for money. The supply of money is determined by the actions of the Federal Reserve System. The demand for money at *a given interest rate* rises with the level of income and the level of wealth. As income and wealth grow, both businesses and households want more money for (a) day-to-day transactions, (b) contingencies, and (c) as a safe element in their stock of wealth.

The amount of money people want to hold at a given *level of income and wealth* declines as the interest rate rises. When interest rates rise, businesses and households find it worthwhile to hold substitutes for money, such as saving deposits, instead of holding demand deposits and currency.

The level of interest rates influences the level of investment. A rise in interest rates discourages investment and a fall in interest rates stimulates investment expenditures. The rate of investment expenditures is a major determinant of level GNP.

To attain a full-employment GNP, the level of interest rates must be just high enough to bring about a rate of investment equal to the amount the public wishes to save at a full-employment GNP. (Saving includes government saving, which may be positive or negative.)

If we are to achieve a full-employment level of GNP, the money supply must equal the amount the public wishes to hold at the level of interest rates required to generate enough investment to absorb full-employment saving.

If the public wishes to save more at a given level of income, the money supply must increase to reduce interest rates and increase the rate of investment.

The full-employment level of income grows from year to year as the labor force and its productivity grows. The demand for money grows with income and, ordinarily, the supply of money must also grow. Otherwise, interest rates would tend to rise and check the growth of investment.

Many factors influence the level of GNP. A rise in GNP may be stimulated by an increase in investment opportunities, by an increase in government expenditures, or by a reduction in tax rates. An increase in income from any of those sources sets off a multiplier process. At the same time, the rise in income is a further stimulus to investment. If the money supply does not increase, the increase in interest rates acts as a brake which slows or stops the growth of income by depressing investment.

On the other hand, an increase in the money supply can stimulate investment and cause a rise in income. Thus monetary policy can be used either to check or to encourage the growth of demand.

7

MONETARY POLICY IN PRACTICE

In Chapter 3 we showed how the Federal Reserve can control the supply
of money by means of its control over required reserve ratios and the volume
of bank reserves. The Federal Reserve System, you will recall, was brought
into existence as a solution to the monetary problems of the national banking
system. To that end it was granted wide powers: to issue currency, to buy
and sell securities, to lend to member banks at varying interest rates, and
to vary reserve requirements. Those powers enable the Federal Reserve

System to control the money supply. The System was supposed to act as a shock absorber—to absorb or offset the impact of various factors such as seasonal variations in demand for currency which had hitherto disturbed the banking system. It was widely believed that the banking panics of the pre-World War I period were a major cause of economic instability and that those panics were caused by the mechanical defects of the national banking system. The basic notion was that the Federal Reserve System could "keep money out of the way."

But "keeping money out of the way" has not proved to be enough. Even when there are no undesirable fluctuations in bank reserves, and even assuming that the causes of bank failures in the 'thirties have been removed, problems remain. There is no doubt that undesirable changes in bank reserves and bank failures contributed greatly to economic instability in the past. But plenty of causes of instability remain.

Private investment demand is still influenced by changes in techniques, the rate of development of new products, and changing locational factors. Moreover, because the rate of investment is influenced by the level of profits and the rate of capacity utilization, any rapid increase in income tends to generate further increases in investment. On the other hand, investment creates capacity, and investment will tend to decline if income does not grow to keep pace with the capacity being created. Variations in government expenditures may sometimes offset other sources of variations in income, but at times changes in government expenditures (e.g., those due to wars) may be destabilizing in themselves. Consumer expenditures tend to follow changes in income so that variations in government expenditures and private investment have a multiplied effect on total income and expenditures. But at times there are booms and slumps in durable-goods expenditures, which are an independent source of instability.

Under the impact of these forces, the rate of change of total expenditure for goods and services tends to vary widely from year to year. When expenditures grow slowly, the rate of increase of output is also slow and falls below the rate of growth of potential output. Then, idle capacity accumulates, and the rate of unemployment rises. Suppose, on the other hand, that expenditure rises more rapidly than the rate of growth of potential output. Then prices will rise—unless, of course, unemployment is high.[1] Moreover, rising prices and a rate of growth of output which cannot be sustained in the long run may lead to speculative investment based on unrealistic assumptions about future profits. The inevitable collapse of a speculative investment boom is likely to have an adverse effect on the whole economy, including sectors which are not involved in the boom.

Everyone agrees that the objective of monetary policy should be to reduce the instability caused by the factors just mentioned. When expenditures for goods and services are falling, or rising too slowly, monetary policy

---

[1] Another book in this Series, *National Income Analysis,* by C. L. Schultze, deals with these problems.

should be used to encourage investment and increase the rate of growth of expenditure. When, on the other hand, expenditure is growing too rapidly, monetary policy should be used to brake expenditures.

So far so good, but there the agreement ends. People disagree about the importance of inflation and about the extent to which it can be influenced by changes in aggregate demand. They disagree about the degree of danger from speculative booms. And in periods of high unemployment people disagree about the extent to which unemployment can be influenced by changes in aggregate demand. Everyone is "for all the good things and against all the bad things," but that does not help much. We will discuss some of these issues later. Now we want to concentrate on another range of questions. How has Federal Reserve policy operated in recent years, and what effect on economic activity has it had?

Organization and Decision-Making

The Federal Reserve System influences economic activity through the use of three major policy instruments each controlled in a different way. These instruments are:
1. Varying required reserve ratios
2. Open-market operations
3. Varying the discount rate.

Reserve requirements are changed infrequently. They must be the same in all districts for banks of a given class. Reserve requirements are determined by the Board of Governors of the Federal Reserve System.

Open-market operations are carried on continuously. In order to offset currency and gold movements and other factors affecting bank reserves, the system must buy or sell securities almost every day. Decisions on the objectives of open-market operations are made by the Federal Open Market Committee (F.O.M.C.). This committee consists of the seven members of the Board of Governors, the president of the Federal Reserve Bank of New York, and the presidents of 4 of the other reserve banks in rotation. The F.O.M.C. usually meets every 3 weeks. The committee considers the economic outlook and decides whether open-market operations should aim at making credit a little cheaper and easier to get or a little more expensive and hard to get. Their decision is summed up in a directive to the New York Federal Reserve Bank. The New York Federal Reserve Bank makes the actual purchases and sales indicated by the F.O.M.C. There is a daily telephone consultation between the staff of the New York Federal Reserve Bank and the staff of the Board.

Discount rates are set by the directors of the 12 Federal Reserve Banks. But the rates they set must be approved by the Board of Governors. Usually, all the banks change their rates at once (or within a few days), but occasionally one of the banks may lag behind the others.

The Cyclical Pattern of Federal Reserve Policy

Broadly speaking, the Federal Reserve System has pursued, during the last decade, a policy aimed at moderating the swings in economic activity. This policy has been described as one of "leaning against the breeze." Once the Board of Governors has become convinced that a recession is impending or underway, it has taken measures to increase the money supply in order to increase (or check the decline in) expenditures on goods and services by making credit readily and cheaply available. On the other hand, during the upswings of 1954-1957 and 1958-1960, the system aimed, by its own account, at checking the rate of growth of expenditures in order to prevent inflation and the development of an unstable speculative boom. In those instances it used its powers to reduce the availability and raise the cost of credit.

During the upswing from 1961-1963 Federal Reserve policy reflected the fact that though income was growing, unemployment remained high and prices were stable. Bank reserves continued to increase through the first 3 years of the upswing.

POLICY ACTIONS IN RECESSION

Federal Reserve policy was clear-cut and easy to follow during the recessions of 1953-1954, 1957-1958, and 1960-1961. In each of those periods the discount rate was reduced several times; required reserve ratios were reduced 3 times in each of the three recession periods. Open-market operations were used to offset other factors affecting reserves but were not used as the primary instrument in encouraging increases in the money supply.

POLICY DURING UPSWINGS

During the upswings of 1954-1957 and 1958-1960, Federal Reserve policy assumed a quite different character. The discount rate was raised several times in each of these periods to keep it above rising market interest rates and so help to limit member-bank borrowing. Required reserve ratios were left unchanged. Open-market operations were largely used to offset the effects of gold outflows in the later period, as well as a steady increase in currency in circulation. But the net effect of open-market operations, together with the other factors mentioned, was to reduce the bank reserves by only a small amount.

The Effect of Federal Reserve Policy on Money Supply

The policy actions described above influenced the money supply in the way you might expect from what you have learned in Chapters 3 and 4. In each of the recessions demand deposits expanded rapidly.

However, the expansion was not proportional to the amount of reserves provided through open-market operations and reductions in reserve requirements. At the onset of each of the recessions, member banks were heavily indebted to the Federal Reserve Banks. When additional reserves were made available, the banks which were indebted used part of their reserve gains to repay the Federal Reserve Banks. In addition, some country banks allowed their excess reserves to increase during the downswing (see Fig. 20). Thus the expansion in demand deposits was not so large as one would expect on the basis of calculations which neglect changes in member-bank borrowing and excess reserves.

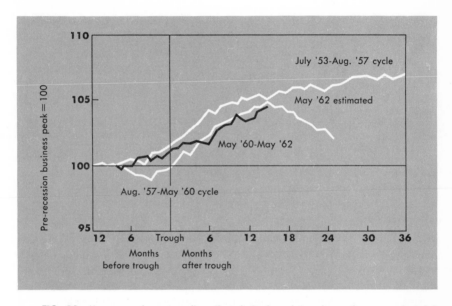

FIG. 19 Money supply, seasonally adjusted. Peak and trough months were selected by National Bureau of Economic Research. (Source: *Federal Reserve Bulletin*, September, 1962.)

During the upswings of 1954-1957 and 1958-1960, the money supply expanded somewhat in spite of the fact that reserves were being drawn away from the banking system. That was possible because banks reduced their excess reserves and borrowed more from the Federal Reserve Banks.

Interest-Rate Movements

Interest rates in the last few years have followed a clearly marked cyclical pattern, declining during recessions and rising during booms. The pattern is readily explained by the movements of GNP and the money supply. During recessions the money supply rose relative to expenditures.

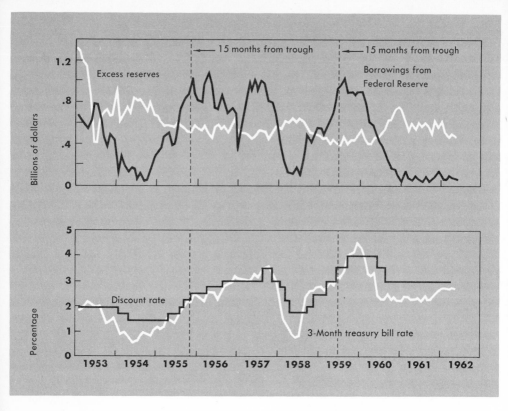

FIG. 20 Excess reserves, borrowings and interest rates. (Source: St. Louis Federal Reserve Bank, *Monthly Review*, July, 1962.)

When the reserve position of banks was improved, banks bid for securities until some individuals found it worthwhile to hold on to money instead of securities.

During the upswings the money supply increased slowly and the GNP rose relative to the money supply. Businesses and households held more money to carry on an increased volume of business. Interest rates had to rise until those people who least needed money were induced to buy securities and turn their money over to people who most needed it and were willing to pay for it.

Bank Loans and Investments

The managements of commercial banks have had plenty of problems in recent years. They have had to keep adjusting their policies in response to changes in Federal Reserve policy and variations in loan demand.

During recession periods banks generally repaid their indebtedness to the Federal Reserve and acquired large amounts of state and local securities. In 1958 and 1960 the increase in assets permitted by reductions in reserve ratios was swelled by the increase in savings deposits that occurred during the period when interest rates on bonds were low. Commercial and industrial loans, of course, declined somewhat during the recessions, as did consumer loans.

Bank managements suffered their real headaches during the periods of increasing business activity in 1954-1957 and 1958-1960. They began the upswing periods in a fairly strong position. They were generally out of debt to the Reserve Banks and had large portfolios of United States securities which could be readily sold without loss. But as the upswing in business activity developed, banks found themselves faced with an intense demand for credit and experienced considerable difficulty in accommodating their customers. The expansion in loan demand reflected the high rate of inventory investment and the increased purchases of automobiles and other consumer durables.

To take care of increasing loan demand, commercial banks sold $10 billion worth of United States securities between 1954 and 1957 and $7 billion worth during 1959. Each loan made by a bank created a new demand deposit, while each sale of a government security extinguished a deposit. Thus the extension of loans and the sale of securities balanced, leaving deposits the same.

But at the time, the banking system as a whole was losing reserves as a result of Federal Reserve action and the other factors that affect reserves. The banks which suffered a net loss of reserves then used excess reserves if they had any or borrowed from the Federal Reserve. During 1955 member banks increased their indebtedness to the Federal Reserve Banks by $600 million and reduced excess reserves by over $100 million. Borrowing declined slightly during 1956 but rose again in 1957.

Late in 1955, many banks, particularly those in New York and other large cities, had borrowed virtually to the limit from their Federal Reserve Banks. These same banks were the ones that had drawn down their portfolio of short-term securities most heavily. Indeed, if they had had a large amount of short-term securities, they probably would have sold them rather than borrow from the Federal Reserve Banks. Banks in New York were faced with a rapidly growing loan demand and more or less static deposits. (The large New York city banks actually lost deposits, while suburban banks gained deposits.) These banks quickly used up their holdings of short-term securities and got themselves into debt with the Federal Reserve Bank. They then found it necessary to become extremely selective in granting loans.

Credit Rationing

We know all about the loans that banks make, but we don't know much about the ones they don't make. Loans expanded so greatly during the 1954-1957 period that some people felt that the "tight money policy" of the Federal Reserve was having no effect on the volume of credit extended and therefore no effect on the rate of spending. There is, however, a substantial amount of evidence which indicates that the growth of bank loans was restricted during the tight-money period. Much of this evidence consists of casual comment, such as the following quote from *U. S. News and World Report* in September, 1956:

> Money is very tight. Loans cost more even for the best-known companies, are harder to arrange, especially for concerns that are not regular borrowers. Mortgages for houses are the hardest type of loan to line up.

Hundreds of similar statements can be found in the financial press during 1956 and 1957.

Somewhat more cogent evidence is given by a survey taken by the American Bankers Association in May, 1957. Close to 80 per cent of the bankers said that they had become more selective in their lending policies since 1955. Asked in what way they had become more selective, the most frequent factor, mentioned by two-thirds of the bankers, was that they were applying "stricter credit reviews." More than half said they were giving increased consideration to past relationships with loan applicants, and 2 out of 5 were paying more attention to the willingness of applicants to maintain "good balances." About 40 per cent also mentioned requiring faster repayment, while one-quarter indicated that they were scaling down loan requests. One economist who worked on the replies to the survey estimated that according to the bankers the volume of loans might have been $2 to $4 billion higher had there been no credit restraint. It does not follow, of course, that expenditures for goods and services were reduced that much. Some of the would-be borrowers raised funds elsewhere; some of them reduced their holdings of cash and securities and went ahead with their expenditure plans. But some expenditures were undoubtedly cut off.

Interest Rates and Spending

The interest-rate movements induced by changing Federal Reserve policy had an appreciable influence on investment expenditures. The obvious effects were felt in the residential construction field.

In each of the three recessions, monetary policy was noticeably successful in bringing about an increase in residential construction. In each case the rise in residential construction played a major part in bringing about and continuing the recovery. The sequence of events was as follows:

1. Federal Reserve action (mainly reductions in reserve requirements) enabled banks to buy bonds and expand the money supply.

2. Interest rates on bonds declined.

3. Households reduced their bond purchases and increased their rate of acquisition of savings deposits and shares.

4. The decline in bond yields made mortgages, and particularly FHA

and VA mortgages with ceiling interest rates, more attractive to mortgage lenders.

5. These lenders also had more funds available to invest.

6. The increased availability of mortgage funds—especially funds for low down-payment mortgages—made it easy to sell houses, and builders increased their activity.

Some time elapsed between the change in monetary policy and its effect on residential construction. It took some time for Federal Reserve action to influence interest rates, more time for mortgage lenders to respond to the change, and still more time for builders to get into action. It took from 6 months to a year from the moment of a marked change in monetary policy until a significant rise in residential construction occurred. Another 6 to 9 months elapsed before residential construction reached its peak.

Interest rates began to rise during the recoveries of 1954 and 1958 and presently reversed the forces which had stimulated residential construction. Rising interest rates on bonds caused households to use a larger proportion of their funds to buy bonds and a smaller proportion for savings deposits and shares. At the same time, lenders found bonds relatively more attractive. Low down payments and insured and guaranteed mortgages became difficult to get. During the 1954-1957 upturn of the business cycle, residential construction reached a peak in the first quarter of 1956 and slowly declined until after the change in monetary policy in late 1957. During the 1958-1960 upturn, residential construction reached a peak in early 1959 and then declined until late 1960.

During the recovery from the 1960-1961 recession, residential construction rose as before, but monetary policy remained easy for a long time after the recovery began. Residential construction continued at a high level through 1963.

The movements of residential construction provide an ideal example of the influence of monetary policy on investment expenditures. When the Federal Reserve increased the money supply, the rate of residential construction increased. When the Federal Reserve put a brake on the money supply, the rate of construction slowed down.

The effects of interest-rate changes in other areas of investment were much less marked. As we have already noted, there is statistical evidence to show that plant and equipment investment does respond to changes in interest rates, although there is a good deal of controversy generally about the magnitude of the impact of interest rates on investment. Most economists agree that plant and equipment investment is signficantly influenced by changes in monetary policy. They also agree that it takes a fairly long time for the effect of a change in monetary policy to work itself out. Just as in the housing case, there is a lag between the initiation of a policy change and its effect on interest rates. There is an additional lag between changes in interest rates and changes in business decisions. The expenditures resulting from an investment decision are spread out over a long time—3 years or more in the case of large new plants. The *average* lag between an investor's decision to invest or spend appears to be about a year. The lag between an investor's decisions and the productive activity of producers is probably somewhat shorter.

Although it takes a long time for the full effects of monetary policy to work themselves out, some of the effects are felt fairly quickly so that changes in monetary policy do contribute something to the recovery of plant and equipment investment during recessions. And since prosperous periods have lasted longer than recessions, it has been possible for restrictive monetary policy to cause a significant slowing down of plant and equipment investment during the upswing of the cycle.

During the post-war period, changes in monetary policy have exercised a significant influence on the course of economic activity. Monetary policy undoubtedly played a substantial role in generating recovery from the recessions of 1954, 1958, and 1960. And the experiences of 1956-1957 and 1959 demonstrated the power of monetary policy to check the growth of expenditures during a boom.

The actions of the Federal Reserve System have been the subject of much debate in the last few years. The Board of Governors has been praised by some for checking inflation and speculation in boom periods and thus assisting recovery from the slumps. Others have contended that excessively tight money *caused* the slumps. Some economists think the money supply was expanded too much during recessions and controlled too tightly during booms. The expansion during the slumps, they argue, was contributing to inflation long after the slump was over. And they contend that the effects of restrictive policy are felt long after the need for it is over. Those economists feel that we would do well or better if we just expanded the money supply steadily and did not attempt to control business cycles. Most economists, however, think that monetary policy must be adapted to the changing circumstances of the economy.

Limits to the Power of Monetary Policy

Some people would like to rely on monetary policy as the primary instrument for controlling aggregate demand. They would like to see policy decisions which influence demand taken out of the political arena. Perhaps even more important, they would like to find a way to disconnect decisions about taxes and expenditures from the issues of unemployment and inflation. Fiscal orthodoxy in terms of an annually balanced budget, or at least a budget balanced at a full-employment level of income, would then be possible.

Can we rely on monetary policy to do the whole job of keeping the economy on an even keel? Monetary policy can do a good deal to offset variations in private investment demand, but it cannot do everything. For several years during the Great Depression of the 1930's monetary conditions were as "easy" as possible. After 1934 interest rates fell to the lowest level in history, banks were almost completely out of debt, and member banks had huge amounts of excess reserves. Few people believe that more could have been done to make credit cheaper or more readily available.[2]

In spite of the very easy credit conditions existing from 1934 to 1940, however, private investment did not recover enough to produce full employment. "Hard cases make bad law." Certainly there were all sorts of peculiar circumstances during the 1930's. The experience does not demonstrate that monetary policy is a weak instrument. It only shows that there is some limit to its powers. This is not surprising. There is no reason to expect that there will always be enough private investment to absorb any volume of full-employment savings even under the easiest monetary conditions. When private investment demand is weak, it may be necessary to use fiscal policy to reduce full-employment savings while we also use monetary policy to raise investment.

Monetary policy has its practical limits in the other direction too. There is no doubt that with sufficiently large open-market sales the Federal Reserve could reduce investment by any amount that seemed advisable. But if the system had to act on too large a scale or too rapidly, its efforts at control might produce a financial panic.

Monetary policy is a powerful and useful instrument of economic policy, but it cannot solve all the problems of the economy.

Summary

Federal Reserve policy has been directed toward assisting recovery from recessions by making credit easily and cheaply available. During the upswings of 1954-1957 and 1958-1960, monetary policy was aimed at restricting the rate of growth of demand to prevent further inflation. In the 1961-1963 upswing, unemployment has remained high and prices stable in spite of the growth of income. Monetary policy has been relatively easy during this period.

The course of monetary policy and its effects during recessions can be summarized as follows:

1. Recognition by the Board of Governors and the Federal Open Market Committee that a recession has begun or is impending.
2. Use of the three major instruments of Federal Reserve policy to ease credit conditions:
    a. open-market purchases of securities.
    b. reduction in the discount rate.
    c. reduction in reserve requirements.

[2] Some writers contend that required reserves should not have been increased in 1937. They contend that the banks wanted the very large volume of excess reserves they held. And they argue that the increase in required reserves contributed substantially to the slump of 1938.

Of course, the monetary authorities do not do everything at once. As the recession proceeds, they take first one action then another to ease credit conditions. Their actions may be spread out over several months.

3. The response of banks to Federal Reserve actions:
   a. repayment of debt to Federal Reserve banks.
   b. purchases of securities and consequent increases in demand deposits.
   c. increased willingness to lend.
4. Decline in interest rates as result of 3b.
5. Increased flow of funds into saving deposits and shares.
6. Reduction in cost and increase in availability of mortgage credit.
7. Increased rate of residential construction.
8. Increase in other types of investment expenditure as a consequence of lower interest rates and ready availability of bank loans.

During the upswings of 1954-1957 and 1958-1960 monetary events followed a different course.

1. The scope of open-market operations was limited.
2. Loan demand grew strongly during the upswing and banks sold large amounts of United States securities while increasing their loans.
3. Many banks with expanding loan demand had chronic difficulty in maintaining the reserve position required by law. Though they sold securities, they also borrowed from the Federal Reserve.
4. The money supply expanded somewhat on the basis of borrowed reserves.
5. Increasing indebtedness to the Federal Reserve and the sale of holdings of short-term securities forced many banks to become more selective in granting loans.
6. GNP rose faster than the money supply; and interest rates rose.
7. Rising interest rates reduced the rate of expenditure on residential construction.
8. Rising interest rates and bank credit rationing checked the expansion of other types of investment.

During the post-war period, monetary policy has demonstrated its power to influence the economy. But the experience of the Great Depression of the 1930's shows that that power is not unlimited.

8

MONEY AND THE GOALS OF ECONOMIC POLICY

The experience of the last few years has demonstrated that monetary policy can play an important role in controlling the level of national income and the rate of investment. But that very success has made the use of monetary policy a focus of controversy. The more effective a policy instrument, the more important it is to use it for the right objectives.

The Federal Reserve System has been concerned with four major objectives of economic policy: (1) full employment; (2) price stability;

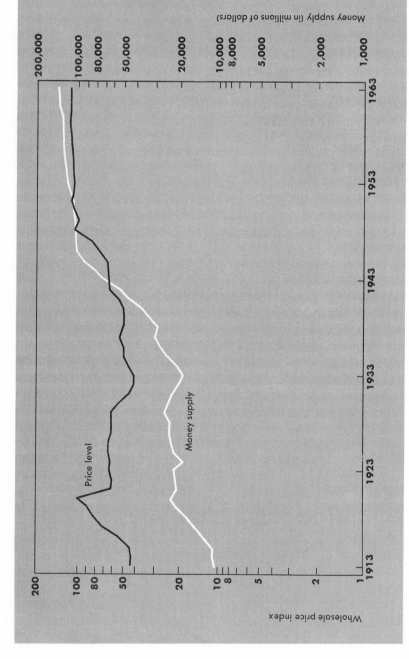

FIG. 21   Deposits adjusted and currency outside banks: 1892-1957; and wholesale price indexes (BLS), by major product group: 1913-1957. (Source: Historical Statistics of U.S.)

(3) economic growth; and (4) a satisfactory balance of payments. To some extent measures taken to achieve one of those objectives assist in the achievement of others. But at times the different objectives appear to be in conflict with one another. Can we have full employment and price stability at the same time? Do monetary measures required to maintain a satisfactory balance of payments lower the rate of growth? These questions have vexed economists and government officials for years and continue to do so.

We have already considered the impact of monetary policy on the level of national income and the level of unemployment. In this chapter we will consider the influence of monetary policy on the price level, on the rate of growth of potential output, and on the balance of payments. At the same time, we will note the points at which the different objectives of policy come into conflict, and some proposals for resolving the conflicts.

Money and Inflation

There is a long tradition of association between money and inflation.

Many people assume that printing paper money or debasing a metallic coinage automatically leads to inflation. In recent discussions of the 1964 tax reduction, it has been argued that inflation would result if the government deficit were to be financed by an expansion of bank credit.

The most spectacular inflations have occurred during wars. Figure 21 shows that in those wartime inflations the quantity of money also increased rapidly. Some economists regard this as evidence of a regular connection between changes in the quantity of money and changes in prices. Other statistical evidence can be cited to support the view that prices rise more rapidly when the money supply increases rapidly than when it does not. The economists who emphasize the connection between money and prices uphold a modern version of the "quantity theory of money" mentioned in Chapter 6. But except for the wartime periods, the connection between changes in money supply and changes in prices is neither strong nor obvious. Most economists agree that there is a connection between changes in money supply and changes in prices, but only an indirect one. They believe that: (1) the money supply influences expenditures for goods and services, and (2) the rate of expenditure for goods and services influences the movement of prices.

We have already considered the influence of money on GNP at length. Let us now turn to the link between GNP and prices.

GNP and Prices

There is a connection between the growth of GNP expenditures, the growth of potential output, and changes in the price level. *If* the growth of output resulting from an increased money supply or any other factor tending to increase GNP expenditures is greater than the growth of potential output, prices will tend to rise. There are several reasons for this relationship.

1. Employment will rise as output increases, although shortages of labor may develop in some labor markets even though unemployment exists elsewhere. Wages will tend to rise. But obviously the tendency for wages to rise will be stronger if unemployment were low at the start rather than high.

2. Profits will rise and employers will find it easier to grant wage increases.

3. A reduction in unemployment will strengthen the bargaining position of unions.

4. Capacity will be better utilized. Competition for additional sales will be less intense. Business firms will find it easy to raise profit margins and to "pass on" wage increases in the form of price increases.

Monetary Policy and Control of Inflation

Monetary policy can be used to check inflation. When expenditures for goods and services grow faster than potential output and the economy is near full employment, prices tend to rise. If the monetary authorities reduce the supply of money, or even fail to increase it, the increasing demand for money will force up interest rates. The rise in interest rates will reduce the rate of growth of demand. If the monetary brake is applied strongly enough, the rate of growth of demand may become less than the rate of growth of potential output. Unemployment will rise, excess capacity will grow, and prices will stop rising.

We can put the matter in another way. It is certainly possible for prices to rise somewhat without an increase in the money supply. And it is possible to have a large increase in the money supply with little or no increase in prices. But it is very difficult to envisage a really large-scale inflation without a substantial increase in money.

A rapid rise in prices requires a rapid rise in expenditures. In order for expenditures to rise rapidly, while the money supply is constant or rising slowly, the velocity of money must rise rapidly. Velocity does change but it never seems to change more than a few percentage points per year. We can be confident, therefore, that if we can control the money supply we can prevent rapid inflations.

Full Employment with Price Stability

In the years before 1957 most people were well satisfied with the level of unemployment. Even a 4 per cent rate of unemployment seems wastefully high, but the 4 per cent figure was generally regarded as acceptable. But when we had "full employment," prices were rising. In the years since 1957 prices have been reasonably stable but the level of unemployment has averaged over 5 per cent. Must we choose between full employment and price stability? This is what the evidence seems to show.

Of course, one can argue that we have finally beaten the "inflation psychology" which ruled after the end of World War II. Maybe prices would not rise if we got back to full employment. We have no real basis for judgment until we get back to full employment.

If prices should rise significantly when we get back to full employment, what can be done about it? We can either try to live with inflation or try to live with unemployment. Neither of these choices seems to be very attractive. Alternatively, we can try to improve our labor markets—retraining displaced workers, improving the efficiency of the United States Employment Service, assisting workers to migrate from depressed areas, and so on. And we can try to make collective bargaining reflect the national interest in price stability. Certainly there are lots of things to be tried before we decide that we must make the choice between too much unemployment or too much inflation.

Monetary Policy and the Balance of Payments

Until recently, decisions about monetary and fiscal policy have turned entirely on domestic issues. We have been fortunate in our ability to neglect balance-of-payments problems in making our choices. But we are an important international trading nation. And for years many countries have held reserves in the form of dollar bank balances or short-term United States securities. Since the Treasury stands willing to sell gold for dollars, a dollar (until recently at least) has been deemed as good as gold.

The United States has sold more goods and services than it has bought abroad for many years. But we have also made large foreign investments, paying for foreign securities with dollars. And American firms have been building plants abroad and paying for them with dollars. In addition, our military expenditures abroad run to $3 billion annually and we expend another $3 billion a year in foreign aid.

Every time an American buys foreign goods or uses foreign services we pay dollars to foreigners. When we buy securities or make military expenditures abroad, we pay dollars to foreigners. We don't ship them dollar bills. Americans write checks on their bank balances and the credit on the books of an American bank is given to foreigners. Most foreign individuals or businessmen who receive dollar balances sell them to their own central bank for their home currency. Foreign central banks then sell dollars to their own citizens who have to make payments in the United States. When foreigners buy goods and services in the United States, the ownership of balances in American banks is transferred back to United States citizens.

If in some particular year we pay foreigners more than they pay us, they realize a net increase in their holdings of dollars. The amount of that net increase is called the balance-of-payments deficit of the United States. Foreign central banks may exchange part of their dollar bank balances for gold by giving the Treasury a check. So the balance-of-payments deficit is the sum of (1) the increase in foreign holdings of dollars, and (2) our sales of gold to foreign central banks. The balance-of-payments deficit is also the excess of all our payments to foreigners over all their payments to us.

The United States has had a balance-of-payments deficit in most years since the end of World War II. The deficit averaged $1 billion per year from 1951 through 1957. But in 1958 the deficit rose to 3.5 billion and, though fluctuating, has averaged over $3 billion per year in the period from 1958 to 1963.

The continuing deficit in the balance of payments has been reflected in a rise in foreign holdings of dollars and a decline in the U. S. gold stock. In 1948 our gold stock stood at $24.4 billion and foreign dollar balances at $6.1 billion. In 1963 our gold stock was less than $16 billion and foreign holdings of dollars had risen to over $24 billion. The continuing decline in gold reserves and the rise in claims against them has raised fears about the ability of the U. S. to maintain the international value of the dollar.

There has been much dispute over the causes of our balance-of-payments deficit. Some have attributed the difficulty to inflation. "We have priced ourselves out of the market," is a frequent comment. Our share of world exports of manufactures has declined, particularly in the fields of steel and machinery, where prices rose most rapidly in the 1954-1957 period. But since 1957 U. S. prices for manufactured good have been relatively stable, whereas European prices have been rising.

Our exports have been held down by other factors besides prices. Some of our best customers—e.g., Canada and Latin America—have been developing slowly. European production has been increasing, so European exporters are in a better position to supply their export markets than they were a few years ago.

But the balance of payments includes other things besides commercial exports and imports. We still sell more abroad than we buy. But our military and foreign-aid expenditures abroad are heavy. Some people believe we should cut these expenditures, but notice that some of our commercial exports result from our aid and military expenditure programs.

Finally, United States firms have been building plants abroad and

United States citizens have been buying foreign securities. The increase in our loans to foreigners arises from the fact that any West European currency can now be converted freely into any other currency. American lenders now consider it safe to lend in Europe and Japan. In addition, United States interest rates have been low relative to foreign rates. And the United States money market is large and well organized. It is easier to borrow a large sum in New York than anywhere else in the world.

All these factors contribute to the balance-of-payments problem. The problem can only be solved by an attack on all the causes.

Traditionally, countries faced with balance-of-payments problems have used monetary policy as a means of eliminating their deficits. The Bank of England raised the discount rate from 5 per cent to 7 per cent in a recent balance-of-payments crisis. A restrictive monetary policy tends to reduce a country's balance-of-payments deficit in three ways: (1) It tends to reduce demand in the country applying it, which in turn tends to reduce the demand for imports as well as for domestic products. (2) The reduction in domestic demand holds down the rate of inflation or reduces prices, which makes imported goods less attractive and makes the deficit country's exports more attractive to foreigners. (3) Higher interest rates make it less attractive for foreigners to borrow in the deficit country and more attractive for them to invest there.

When a country has a balance-of-payments deficit because it has permitted inflation at home, the tight-money solution looks very sensible. But we have had less inflation than most other countries. Our domestic demand position has not been satisfactory for some time.

Conflicts between Balance of Payments and Full Employment

We are faced with another conflict of objectives. We can achieve full employment by the appropriate use of fiscal and monetary policy. An increase in employment and income implies an increase in imports and probably a higher rate of inflation. Both those reactions tend to worsen the balance-of-payments situation. There are some offsetting considerations. An increase in our national income spells high profits and higher prospective returns on investment for U. S. business firms. Prosperity here may induce some American firms to build plants here rather than abroad. And some of our increased imports will come from countries who will buy more from us with the proceeds. It is not certain, therefore, that a rise in our national income will worsen our balance-of-payments position, but many people believe that it will.

Monetary policy along with fiscal policy influences the balance-of-payments position through its effect on national income and thence on imports and the price level. But monetary policy has a special effect on capital movements which enter the balance of payments. Foreigners have found it desirable to borrow in the U. S. for many reasons, but our capital markets are particularly attractive to foreigners when interest rates here are low compared with those abroad. Americans find foreign securities attractive for the same reason.

The Federal Reserve could restrict the growth of the money supply and drive up interest rates here. If that were done to a sufficient extent, foreigners would find it less profitable to borrow here and Americans would find foreign securities less attractive. A restrictive monetary policy would tend to hold down national income and employment. However, that effect could be offset by lower taxes or increasing government expenditures. In other words, the government could lower the full-employment savings rate and raise the level of interest rates, which is consistent with full employment. Such a combination of policies would improve the balance-of-payments position without having an adverse effect on domestic income and employment. Unfortunately, there is a price for everything. An increase in interest rates has an adverse effect on investment and on the long-term growth of output, as we shall see below.

Some people who want full employment and rapid growth would like to solve the balance-of-payments problem by devaluation. They would make the dollar worth less in terms of foreign currencies and so discourage imports and encourage exports. But considerations of international prestige make that solution objectionable. Moreover, we have been trying to encourage an expansion in international trade on the basis of stable exchange rates. An American devaluation would upset all that.

In seeking to avoid the dilemmas posed by the balance of payments, the government has tried a variety of measures. These include a drive to attract tourists, a variety of measures to increase exports, requiring that foreign aid grants and loans be spent in the United States, and arranging the sale of United States military equipment to some of our European allies. In the monetary field the Federal Reserve and Treasury have tried to drive up short-term interest rates to discourage lending abroad while at the same time holding down long-term rates. In 1964 an interest equalization was levied on foreign securities issues in the U. S., but at this writing the balance-of-payments problem remains unsolved.

Monetary Policy and Growth

The potential output of our economy is always growing. It does so because the labor force grows, technology is improved, and capital accumulated. In the early 'sixties concern has developed because growth in demand has not kept pace with potential output. At the same time, however, many people have begun looking for ways to speed up the rate of growth of *potential* output. They hope, first, to get income up to the full-employment level; second, to keep demand growing in pace with potential output; and third, to speed up the growth of potential output.

One way to increase the rate of growth of potential output is to increase the rate of adoption of labor-saving techniques. (The unemployment thus created would have to be absorbed by an appropriate increase in demand.) To speed up the rate of adoption of labor-saving techniques, it is necessary to increase the rate of investment.

We have some choice about the level of interest rates. If we want to maximize investment for growth, interest rates must be kept at their lowest possible average level. To achieve that level without inducing inflation, we need a suitable fiscal policy, a fiscal policy which generates a high level of total saving—at full employment. More precisely, the full-employment rate of saving should be high enough to equal the full-employment rate of investment generated by the monetary conditions we desire. If we want easy money to foster growth, we must be willing to pay the price by saving enough to provide for the investment we want.

Notice, however, that the combination of fiscal and monetary policy suitable for encouraging investment (i.e., tight fiscal policy—easy money) is precisely the opposite of the one suggested for solving the balance-of-payments problem.

Conclusion

Money has caused problems ever since it came into use, but the nature of the problems has changed. For a long time, monetary problems arose because the supply of money could not be controlled in a manner consistent with the needs of the economy. With the development of modern central banking and with such safety devices as deposit insurance, we can be fairly sure that money will not cause trouble just because we do not know how to control it. The technical problems of controlling the money supply are largely solved. We now view control of the money supply as a powerful instrument of economic policy, which necessarily raises the problem of the objectives of control. Monetary policy is necessarily concerned with all the major objectives of economic policy, and those objectives are, to some extent, in conflict with one another. Difficult choices must be made and controversy over any decision reached by the monetary authorities is inevitable.

Some people are prepared to solve the problems of choice by simply abandoning some policy objectives. Thus there are some people who put price stability and the international position of the dollar before all other objectives. They would choose a combination of monetary and fiscal policy which would insure price stability and eliminate the balance-of-payments deficit.

At the other extreme are those who want full employment and low interest rates (to encourage growth) regardless of the cost in terms of balance-of-payments difficulties or inflation. They are, if pressed, willing to accept devaluation as a solution to the balance-of-payments problem and some form of price and wage control to deal with inflation.

These are some extreme views and they differ primarily in the value judgments people entertain about the importance of unemployment, growth of output, devaluation, inflation, and price control. But people also differ in their analysis of the consequences of the policies advocated. People who are concerned about price stability and the payments deficit often argue that the confidence engendered by a "sound" policy will more than offset the adverse effects of tight money. And they may argue that the unemployed are "unemployable" or nonexistent (challenging the unemployment statistics).

Their opponents often contend that the balance-of-payments deficit will improve in time without special action. They argue that high employment and high growth at home help our international position in certain ways. And, they are optimistic about the prospects of achieving full employment without inflation.

Few people are willing to admit that any one of the four policy goals should be abandoned. The differences in their views are reflected in the things they are willing to take a chance on. Some people want positive action to insure full employment and growth. They are willing to take a chance on the possibility that their analysis of the inflation and balance-of-payments problems is wrong. Others take the reverse position. Most people take some intermediate position. [Actual monetary policy inevitably involves some degree of compromise among the competing policy objectives and some balancing of conflicting judgments on the consequences of alternative policies. Moreover, practical monetary policy is made by the continuous response of the monetary authorities to changing circumstances and changing judgments about future conditions. Faced with a set of conflicting objectives, whose achievement is influenced by a variety of factors, the problem of monetary management is one of continuous adaptation.] There is no magic formula for the problems of monetary control.

Summary

The goals of economic policy include (1) full employment, (2) stable prices, (3) a high rate of growth, and (4) a satisfactory balance-of-payments position. Monetary policy influences the level of employment, the price level, the rate of growth, and the balance of payments. The level of employment is influenced by the level of interest rates and the availability of credit. The rate of increase of prices tends to rise as we approach full employment. Notice that monetary policy influences prices through its influence on employment and capacity utilization. An effort to control inflation by monetary action tends to increase unemployment simultaneously.

Monetary policy influences the balance of payments because low interest rates at home encourage Americans to invest abroad. At the same time, low interest rates tend to increase the rate of investment in plant and equipment in this country and so increase the rate of growth of potential output.

In making monetary policy it is often necessary to choose among conflicting objectives. The conflicts among objectives may be reduced by the use of other policies. Thus the rate of inflation at full employment can be reduced by a variety of measures to improve the operation of our labor markets.

We saw in the last chapter that various combinations of monetary policy and fiscal policy are consistent with full employment. Thus an easy-money policy can be used to foster a high rate of capital formation provided that fiscal policy is used to provide a sufficiently high level of full-employment saving.

For detailed treatments of money and banking, any of the following intermediate textbooks are recommended: William Howard Steiner, *et al., Money and Banking,* 4th ed. (New York: Holt, Rinehart & Winston, 1958); Lester Chandler, *The Economics of Money and Banking,* 3rd ed. (New York: Harper, 1959); George N. Halm, *Economics of Money and Banking* (Homewood, Ill.: Irwin, 1961); Albert B. Hart and Peter B. Kenen, *Money, Debt and Economic Activity,* 3rd ed. (Englewood Cliffs, N. J.: Prentice-Hall, 1961); A. C. L. Day and Sterie T. Beza, *Money and Income* (New York: Oxford University Press, 1960); and Dennis H. Robertson, *Money* (Chicago: University of Chicago Press, 1959).

For readings in a wide variety of topics in money and banking, see Lawrence S. Ritter, *Money and Economic Activity,* 2nd ed. (Boston: Houghton Mifflin, 1961).

On the origins and development of money, see Paul Einzig, *Primitive Money in Its Ethnological, Historical and Economic Aspects* (New York: Humanities Press). A succinct account of American banking history is provided by Bray Hammond, "Historical Introduction," in *Banking Studies,* Board of Governors of the Federal Reserve System, Washington, D.C.: 1941.

On the organization of the Federal Reserve System, see *The Federal Reserve System: Its Structure and Function,* 4th ed., Board of Governors of the Federal Reserve System, Washington, D.C.: 1961. The conduct of open-market operations is described in R. V. Roosa, *Federal Reserve Operations in the Money and Securities Markets,* Federal Reserve Bank of New York, New York, 1956.

For a more detailed analysis of bank management problems, see Roland Robinson, *Management of Bank Funds,* 2nd ed. (New York: McGraw-Hill, 1962). An interesting picture of day-to-day reserve management problems is given in *The Money Side of the Street,* Federal Reserve Bank of New York.

The Commission on Money and Credit has published a series of volumes covering the history, functions and problems of public regulation of the major financial institutions, all published by Prentice-Hall, Inc., Englewood Cliffs, N. J., 1963. Following are the titles: *The Commercial Banking Industry; The Consumer Finance Industry; Life Insurance Companies as Financial Institutions; Management Investment Companies; Mortgage Companies; Mutual Savings Banking; Property and Casualty Insurance Companies; The Savings and Loan Business; Federal Credit Agencies; Federal Credit Programs; Private Capital Markets;* and *Private Financial Institutions.*

For a theoretical view of the role of financial intermediaries, see Edward S. Shaw and John G. Gurley, *Money In a Theory of Finance* (Washington, D.C.: The Brookings Institution, 1960).

The problems of Federal Reserve policy in the early post-World War II years were thoroughly aired in two sets of congressional hearings. See U.S. Congress, Joint Committee on the Economic Report, Subcommittee on Monetary Credit and Fiscal Policy, Hearing, 1949, Statements, 1949, Report, 1950, 81st Congress (commonly called the Douglas Committee Report); and U.S. Congress Joint Economic Committee Subcommittee on General Credit Control and Debt Management, Hearings, Replies to Questions and Other Material. Report, 82nd Congress, 2nd Session, 1952 (Patman Committee).

For a radical critique of all our money institutions, see Milton Friedman, *Program for Monetary Stability* (New York: Fordham University Press, 1959). On the supply of money and changes in prices and output see Friedman's *The Relation of Prices to Economic Stability and Growth,* U.S. Congress Joint Economic Committee, 1958.

Most of the issues in monetary policy are reviewed in the Report of the Commission on Money and Credit.